New Vegetarian Curry Recipes

Veena Chopra

foulsham
LONDON • NEW YORK • TORONTO • SYDNEY

foulsham

Yeovil Road, Slough, Berkshire SL1 4JH

ISBN 0-572-01939-4

Typeset in Great Britain by Encounter Photosetting, Fleet, Hampshire
Printed in Great Britain by St Edmundsbury Press Ltd, Bury St Edmunds, Suffolk.

▼

Contents

Introduction

In India, large numbers of people are vegetarian, and the Indian soil produces a wonderful variety of vegetables. There is therefore lots of experimentation and research into vegetable and vegetarian cooking, especially since even those who do eat meat cannot afford to eat it every day, and often prefer not to eat it when the weather is particularly hot.

So the extent and variety of Indian vegetarian cooking is exciting! You can experiment with all manner of ingredients, following specific recipes while you become familiar with the flavours and techniques of the cookery, and then perhaps even experimenting with your own variations and new dishes.

Above all, food is a social experience; a way of enjoying being with other people and enjoying good food together.

▼

Ingredients

Most of the spices commonly used in Indian cookery are now readily available in supermarkets so that you can gradually build up your collection until you have a comprehensive selection suitable for all the dishes in this book. A few ingredients are slightly less common and you may have to buy them from an Indian food store.

Ajowain: This is available as a seed which tastes strongly of thyme. It is sometimes known as tymol or lovage seed.

Asafoetida: A strong spice often used as a substitute for salt, this is available powdered or in a block.

Beans and Pulses: A variety of beans and pulses are available in Indian food stores. They are usually sold under their Indian names. Always wash and then pick over before use.

Cardamom: Cardamom pods are the dried fruits of a plant from the ginger family. They vary in colour from white to black. The seeds are contained inside the pods.

Citric acid: This is available in Asian stores or health shops.

Cumin: Cumin is used either as whole seed, or the seed is roasted and then ground. It is readily available in supermarkets.

Eno: Indian cooks use the digestive which you can buy at the chemist or supermarket.

Ginger root: Fresh ginger root is readily available in supermarkets and greengrocers. Before use, peel off the thick outer skin and then grate the root.

Ground mango powder: This is available in Asian stores.

Kalonji: Kalonji are onion seeds, which are available in Asian food stores.

Tamarind pulp: This is a sour ingredient which is available as a dried pulp or concentrate. See page 94 on how to reconstitute tamarind pulp.

▼

Notes on the Recipes

1 Follow one set of measurements only, do not mix Metric, Imperial or American.

2 Wash fresh produce before preparation.

3 Spoon measurements are level.

4 A tablespoon is 15 ml; a teaspoon is 5 ml.

5 Adjust spices, seasoning and strongly-flavoured ingredients, such as onions and garlic, to suit your own taste. This is particularly important in Indian cookery, as spices are used in almost all dishes. Try using the minimum quantities until you become familiar with the strengths of various ingredients.

6 If you substitute dried for fresh herbs, use only half the amount specified.

▼

Main Dishes

APPLE CURRY

	ingredients		
Serves 4 - 6	Metric	Imperial	American
Small cooking (tart) apples	6	6	6
Oil for deep–frying			
Oil or ghee	150 ml	¼ pt	⅔ cup
Cumin seeds	5 ml	1 tsp	1 tsp
Medium onions, chopped	2	2	2
Cloves	4	4	4
Peppercorns	4	4	4
Cinnamon stick	2.5 cm	1 in	1 in
Black cardamom pod	1	1	1
Large garlic cloves, chopped	4	4	4
Fresh ginger root, coarsely chopped	2.5 cm	1 in	1 in
Water	450 ml	¾ pt	2 cups
Poppy seeds, finely ground	25 g	1 oz	1 oz
Desiccated coconut, finely ground	75 g	3 oz	¾ cup
Ground coriander	10 ml	2 tsp	2 tsp
Ground turmeric	5 ml	1 tsp	1 tsp
Ground red chilli	2.5 ml	½ tsp	½ tsp
Garam masala	2.5 ml	½ tsp	½ tsp
Salt to taste			

Canned tomatoes	400 g	14 oz	14 oz
Lemon juice	15 ml	1 tbsp	1 tbsp
GARNISH			
Garam masala	2.5 ml	½ tsp	½ tsp
Chopped fresh			
coriander leaves	15 ml	1 tbsp	1 tbsp
Small green chilli,			
chopped	1	1	1

method

1. Peel the apples and remove the pips and core with a sharp knife. Prick the apples all over with a fork then deep-fry in hot oil until golden brown. Drain and reserve.

2. Heat the oil or ghee in a large heavy-based pan and fry the cumin seeds until lightly browned. Add 1 chopped onion and the cloves, peppercorns, cinnamon and cardamon and fry gently over a medium heat until golden brown.

3. Blend the remaining onion, the garlic, ginger and 30 ml/2 tbsp of water to a smooth paste in a blender or food processor. Stir into the pan and fry for 5 minutes.

4. Add the poppy seeds and fry for 2 minutes.

5. Add the coconut and fry for a further few minutes until golden brown.

6. Stir in the coriander, turmeric, chilli, garam masala, salt and tomatoes and fry until all the liquid has been absorbed and the oil appears on the surface of the mixture.

7. Add 45 ml/3 tbsp of water and fry until it is absorbed. Repeat this twice, then add the remaining water and the lemon juice. Bring to the boil, cover and simmer gently for 3 minutes.

8. Pour the sauce into a serving dish and top with the fried apples. Sprinkle over the garnish ingredients and serve hot with rice and a potato or bean dish.

STUFFED OKRA

ingredients

Serves 4 - 6

	Metric	Imperial	American
Ground coriander	30 ml	2 tbsp	2 tbsp
Ground roasted cumin	15 ml	1 tbsp	1 tbsp
Ground mango powder	15 ml	1 tbsp	1 tbsp
or Citric acid	2.5 ml	½ tsp	½ tsp
Garam masala	10 ml	2 tsp	2 tsp
Ground red chilli	5 ml	1 tsp	1 tsp
Ground turmeric	5 ml	1 tsp	1 tsp
Ground ginger	5 ml	1 tsp	1 tsp
Ground mace	2.5 ml	½ tsp	½ tsp
Ground nutmeg	2.5 ml	½ tsp	½ tsp
Small green chilli, finely chopped	1	1	1
Salt to taste			
Small, tender okra, slit lengthways	500 g	18 oz	18 oz
Oil	60 ml	4 tbsp	4 tbsp

⑨

method

1. Mix together all the spices and the chilli and push the stuffing into the slits in the okra.

2. Heat the oil in a heavy-based pan and add the okra. Cover and cook on a low heat for 10 minutes until tender, turning regularly.

3. Serve hot with puri or paratha, rice, lentil and rayta.

AUBERGINE AND POTATO

ingredients

Serves 4

	Metric	Imperial	American
Oil	75 ml	5 tbsp	5 tbsp
Large pinch of asafoetida			
Fenugreek seeds	2.5 ml	½ tsp	½ tsp
Mustard seeds	2.5 ml	½ tsp	½ tsp
Large garlic cloves, crushed	2	2	2
Fresh ginger root	1 cm	½ in	½ in
Small onion, finely chopped	1	1	1
Potato, cut into 2.5 cm/1 in pieces	250 g	9 oz	9 oz
Desiccated coconut	15 ml	1 tbsp	1 tbsp
Aubergine (eggplant), cut into 2.5 cm/ 1 in pieces	250 g	9 oz	9 oz
Ground coriander	5 ml	1 tsp	1 tsp
Ground roasted cumin	5 ml	1 tsp	1 tsp
Garam masala	2.5 ml	½ tsp	½ tsp
Ground red chilli	2.5 ml	½ tsp	½ tsp
Ground turmeric	2.5 ml	½ tsp	½ tsp
Salt to taste			
Canned tomatoes	225 g	8 oz	½ lb
Sugar	15 ml	1 tbsp	1 tbsp
Lemon juice	15 ml	1 tbsp	1 tbsp
GARNISH			
Pinch of garam masala			
Chopped fresh coriander leaves	15 ml	1 tbsp	1 tbsp
Small green chilli, chopped	1	1	1

(10)

| method |

1. Heat the oil in a large heavy-based pan and fry the asafoetida, fenugreek and mustard seeds over a medium heat until the mustard seeds start to crack.

2. Add the garlic, ginger and onion and fry until lightly browned.

3. Add the potato and fry until golden brown.

4. Add the coconut and aubergine and fry for 1 minute.

5. Stir in the coriander, cumin, garam masala, chilli, turmeric and salt. Stir in the tomatoes. Reduce the heat to low, cover and simmer for 20 minutes until the vegetables are tender, stirring occasionally. Add a little water if the mixture becomes too thick.

6. Add the sugar and lemon juice, increase the heat and fry until any remaining liquid has evaporated.

7. Sprinkle with the garnish ingredients and serve hot with dal, rice, rayta, chapati or paratha.

BEANS AND POTATO

Serves 4

ingredients

	Metric	Imperial	American
Oil or ghee	75 ml	5 tbsp	5 tbsp
Mustard seeds	2.5 ml	½ tsp	½ tsp
Cumin seeds	2.5 ml	½ tsp	½ tsp
Large garlic cloves, crushed	2	2	2
Fresh ginger root, finely chopped	2.5 cm	1 in	1 in
Medium onion, finely chopped	1	1	1
Potatoes, cut into 1 cm/½ in pieces	250 g	9 oz	9 oz
Beans, cut into 1 cm/½ in pieces	250 g	9 oz	9 oz
Garam masala	5 ml	1 tsp	1 tsp
Ground coriander	5 ml	1 tsp	1 tsp
Ground roasted cumin	5 ml	1 tsp	1 tsp
Ground red chilli	2.5 ml	½ tsp	½ tsp
Ground turmeric	2.5 ml	½ tsp	½ tsp
Salt to taste			
Canned tomatoes	250 g	9 oz	9 oz
Water	50 ml	2 fl oz	3½ tbsp
Lemon juice	15 ml	1 tbsp	1 tbsp
GARNISH			
Pinch of garam masala			
Small green chilli, chopped	1	1	1

method

1. Heat the oil or ghee in a large heavy-based pan and fry the mustard seeds over a medium heat until they start crackling. Add the cumin seeds and fry until browned.

2. Add the garlic, ginger and onion and fry until lightly browned.

3. Add the potatoes and fry for 5 minutes.

4. Add the beans and fry for 2 minutes.

5. Stir in the garam masala, coriander, cumin, chilli, turmeric, salt, lemon juice, tomatoes and water. Bring to the boil, reduce the heat to low, cover and simmer for 15 minutes until tender, stirring occasionally.

6. Increase the heat and simmer until the remaining liquid has evaporated.

7. Sprinkle over the garnish ingredients and serve hot with onion paratha, puri, dal and rice.

CABBAGE AND PEAS

Serves 4 - 6

(13)

ingredients

	Metric	Imperial	American
Oil or ghee	60 ml	5 tbsp	5 tbsp
Mustard seeds	5 ml	1 tsp	1 tsp
Cumin seeds	5 ml	1 tsp	1 tsp
Large garlic cloves, crushed	2	2	2
Fresh ginger root, finely chopped	1 cm	½ in	½ in
Small onion, finely chopped	1	1	1
Garam masala	5 ml	1 tsp	1 tsp
Ground coriander	5 ml	1 tsp	1 tsp
Ground red chilli	2.5 ml	½ tsp	½ tsp
Ground turmeric	2.5 ml	½ tsp	½ tsp
Salt to taste			
Canned tomatoes	225 g	8 oz	½ lb
Cabbage, shredded	500 g	18 oz	18 oz
Frozen peas, thawed	150 g	5 oz	5 oz
Lemon juice	15 ml	1 tbsp	1 tbsp

GARNISH			
Garam masala	1.5 ml	¼ tsp	¼ tsp
Chopped fresh coriander	15 ml	1 tbsp	1 tbsp
Small green chilli, chopped	1	1	1

method

1. Heat the oil or ghee in a heavy-based pan and fry the mustard seeds over a medium heat until they start crackling. Add the cumin seeds and fry until browned.

2. Add the garlic, ginger and onion and fry until golden brown.

3. Stir in the garam masala, coriander, chilli, turmeric and salt.

4. Stir in the tomatoes and cabbage, cover and simmer over a medium heat for 10 minutes, stirring occasionally.

5. Add the peas and simmer for 5 minutes until the vegetables are tender.

(14)

6. Mix in the lemon juice. Sprinkle over the garnish ingredients and serve hot with dal, rice, rayta and chapati or puri.

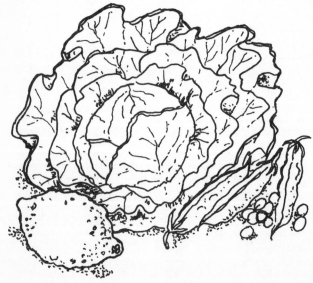

FRIED OKRA

	ingredients		
Serves 4	Metric	Imperial	American
Oil	75 ml	5 tbsp	5 tbsp
Medium onion, finely chopped	3	3	3
Fresh ginger root, finely chopped	2.5 cm	½ in	½ in
Tender okra, cut into 1 cm/½ in round pieces	500 g	18 oz	18 oz
Ground coriander	15 ml	1 tbsp	1 tbsp
Ground roasted cumin	5 ml	1 tsp	1 tsp
Ground turmeric	5 ml	1 tsp	1 tsp
Ground red chilli	2.5 ml	½ tsp	½ tsp
Garam masala	2.5 ml	½ tsp	½ tsp
Salt to taste			
GARNISH			
Garam masala	2.5 ml	½ tsp	½ tsp
Small green chilli, chopped	1	1	1

(15)

method

1. Heat the oil and fry the onion and ginger over a medium heat until lightly browned.

2. Add the okra and fry for 5 minutes.

3. Add the coriander, cumin, turmeric, chilli, garam masala and salt, cover and cook on a low heat for 5-7 minutes until tender, turning continuously.

4. Sprinkle with the garnish ingredients and serve hot with paratha or puri, dal, rayta and rice.

CARROT AND PEAS

Serves 4

ingredients

	Metric	Imperial	American
Oil	60 ml	4 tbsp	4 tbsp
Mustard seeds	5 ml	1 tsp	1 tsp
Cumin seeds	5 ml	1 tsp	1 tsp
Large garlic cloves, crushed	2	2	2
Fresh ginger root, finely chopped	1 cm	½ in	½ in
Small onion, finely chopped	1	1	1
Ground coriander	5 ml	1 tsp	1 tsp
Garam masala	2.5 ml	½ tsp	½ tsp
Ground red chilli	2.5 ml	½ tsp	½ tsp
Ground turmeric	2.5 ml	½ tsp	½ tsp
Salt to taste			
Canned tomatoes	225 g	8 oz	½ lb
Tender small carrots, cut into 2.5 cm/1 in pieces	500 g	18 oz	18 oz
Frozen peas, thawed	250 g	9 oz	9 oz
GARNISH			
Garam masala	2.5 ml	½ tsp	½ tsp
Chopped fresh coriander	15 ml	1 tbsp	1 tbsp
Small green chilli, chopped	1	1	1

16

method

1. Heat the oil in a heavy-based pan and fry the mustard seeds over a medium heat until they start crackling. Add the cumin seeds and fry until lightly browned.

2. Stir in the garlic, ginger and onion and fry over a medium heat until golden brown.

3. Stir in the coriander, garam masala, chilli, turmeric and salt. Stir in the tomatoes and carrots. Reduce the heat to medium-low, cover and cook for 10 minutes until tender, stirring occasionally. Increase the heat and dry off any remaining water.

4. Stir in the peas and cook for a further few minutes until the peas are tender and the oil appears on the surface of the mixture.

5. Sprinkle over the garnish ingredients and serve hot with dal, rice, puri and rayta.

Variation:
Follow the same recipe, substituting turnip for the carrots.

17

CAULIFLOWER IN CORIANDER, MINT AND YOGHURT

Serves 4

ingredients

	Metric	Imperial	American
Large garlic cloves	4	4	4
Fresh ginger root	4 cm	1½ in	1½ in
Medium onion, coarsely chopped	1	1	1
Salt			
Medium cauliflower, cut into florets	1	1	1
Potatoes, cut into 2.5 cm/1 in pieces	250 g	9 oz	9 oz
Natural yoghurt	450 ml	¾ pt	⅔ cup
Chopped fresh coriander	100 g	4 oz	¼ lb
Bunch of fresh mint leaves	25 g	1 oz	1 oz
Oil	90 ml	6 tbsp	6 tbsp
Ghee	90 ml	6 tbsp	6 tbsp
Mustard seeds	5 ml	1 tsp	1 tsp
Cumin seeds	5 ml	1 tsp	1 tsp
Garam masala	5 ml	1 tsp	1 tsp
Ground coriander	5 ml	1 tsp	1 tsp
Ground red chilli	2.5 ml	½ tsp	½ tsp
Ground roasted cumin	2.5 ml	½ tsp	½ tsp
Ground turmeric	2.5 ml	½ tsp	½ tsp
Lemon juice	45 ml	3 tbsp	3 tbsp

18

method

1. Blend the garlic, ginger, onion and a large pinch of salt to a smooth paste in a blender or food processor. Rub on to the cauliflower and potato pieces and leave to marinate for 30 minutes.

2. Blend the yoghurt, coriander and mint to a smooth paste and set aside.

3. Heat the oil in a heavy-based pan and fry the marinated vegetables over a medium heat for about 20 minutes until golden brown. Remove with a slotted spoon and set aside.

4. Heat the ghee in a heavy-based pan and fry the mustard seeds over a medium heat until they start crackling. Add the cumin seeds and fry for a few seconds until lightly browned.

5. Stir in the garam masala, coriander, chilli, cumin, turmeric and a little salt. Stir in the yoghurt paste and bring to the boil.

6. Add the marinated and fried vegetables and cook for 15 minutes until thick.

(19)

7. Stir in the lemon juice and serve hot with plain rice and dal.

FRIED CAULIFLOWER

Serves 4

ingredients

	Metric	Imperial	American
Large cauliflower	1	1	1
Oil for deep-frying			
Oil or ghee	30 ml	2 tbsp	2 tbsp
Mustard seeds	5 ml	1 tsp	1 tsp
Onion seeds	5 ml	1 tsp	1 tsp
Cumin seeds	5 ml	1 tsp	1 tsp
Ground coriander	5 ml	1 tsp	1 tsp
Garam masala	5 ml	1 tsp	1 tsp
Ground roasted cumin	5 ml	1 tsp	1 tsp

Ground ginger	2.5 ml	½ tsp	½ tsp
Ground red chilli	2.5 ml	½ tsp	½ tsp
Ground turmeric	2.5 ml	½ tsp	½ tsp
Salt to taste			
Lemon juice	15 ml	1 tbsp	1 tbsp
Sugar	15 ml	1 tbsp	1 tbsp
GARNISH			
Garam masala	1.5 ml	¼ tsp	¼ tsp
Chopped fresh coriander	15 ml	1 tbsp	1 tbsp
Small green chilli, chopped	1	1	1

method

1. Cut the cauliflower into 2.5 cm/1 in florets. Peel the stems thinly and slice 5 mm/¼ in thick.

2. Heat the oil and deep-fry the cauliflower until golden brown. Drain and set aside.

3. Heat the oil in a heavy-based pan and fry the mustard and onion seeds over a medium heat until they start crackling. Add the cumin seeds and fry until lightly browned.

4. Add the coriander, garam masala, cumin, ginger, chilli, turmeric and salt. Stir in the cauliflower. Reduce the heat to low and cook for 10 minutes.

5. Stir in the lemon juice and sugar and cook for a further 2 minutes.

6. Sprinkle over the garnish ingredients and serve hot with puri, dal, rayta and biryani.

POTATO SUKHÉ

Serves 4

ingredients

	Metric	Imperial	American
Oil	60 ml	4 tbsp	4 tbsp
Pinch of asafoetida			
Onion seeds	5 ml	1 tsp	1 tsp
Medium onion, finely chopped	1	1	1
Potatoes, cooked and diced	500 g	18 oz	18 oz
Ground coriander	10 ml	2 tsp	2 tsp
Ground roasted cumin	5 ml	1 tsp	1 tsp
Garam masala	2.5 ml	½ tsp	½ tsp
Ground ginger	2.5 ml	½ tsp	½ tsp
Ground red chilli	2.5 ml	½ tsp	½ tsp
Ground turmeric	2.5 ml	½ tsp	½ tsp
Salt to taste			
GARNISH			
Garam masala	2.5 ml	½ tsp	½ tsp
Chopped fresh coriander	15 ml	1 tbsp	1 tbsp

(21)

method

1. Heat the oil and fry the asafoetida until it starts sizzling. Add the onion seeds and fry for 5 seconds. Add the onion and fry until lightly browned.

2. Stir in the potato pieces and fry for 5 minutes.

3. Stir in the coriander, cumin, garam masala, ginger, chilli, turmeric and salt and fry over a low heat for 3 minutes.

4. Sprinkle over the garnish ingredients and serve hot with dal, potatoes and peas, and puri or chapati.

KHADI WITH TARKA

Serves 4

ingredients

	Metric	Imperial	American
KHADI			
Gram flour, sifted	25 g	1 oz	¼ cup
Garam masala	2.5 ml	½ tsp	½ tsp
Ground ginger	2.5 ml	½ tsp	½ tsp
Ground red chilli	2.5 ml	½ tsp	½ tsp
Ground turmeric	2.5 ml	½ tsp	½ tsp
Salt to taste			
Natural yoghurt	450 ml	⅔ pt	2 cups
PAKORA			
Gram flour, sifted	100 g	4 oz	1 cup
Garam masala	5 ml	1 tsp	1 tsp
Ground red chilli	2.5 ml	½ tsp	½ tsp
Ajowain	2.5 ml	½ tsp	½ tsp
Small onions, thinly sliced	2	2	2
Salt to taste			
Oil	15 ml	1 tbsp	1 tbsp
Water	100 ml	3½ fl oz	6½ tbsp
Oil for frying			
Oil	60 ml	4 tbsp	4 tbsp
Large pinch of asafoetida			
Cumin seeds	5 ml	1 tsp	1 tsp
Water	1 l	1⅔ pts	4¼ cups
TARKA			
Ghee	90 ml	6 tbsp	6 tbsp
Mustard seeds	2.5 ml	½ tsp	½ tsp
Small onion, finely chopped	1	1	1
Garam masala	5 ml	1 tsp	1 tsp
Chopped fresh coriander	45 ml	3 tbsp	3 tbsp
Small green chilli, chopped	1	1	1

method

1. Place the gram flour in a bowl and stir in the spices. Gradually blend in the yoghurt.

2. To make the pakora, stir together the gram flour, garam masala, chilli, ajowain, onions and salt. Gradually pour in the oil and water and blend to a smooth batter.

3. Heat the oil in a deep pan over a medium-high heat. Fry tablespoonfuls of the batter until golden brown on both sides. Drain and set aside.

4. Heat the oil in a heavy-based pan and fry the asafoetida over a medium heat until it starts sizzling. Add the cumin seeds and fry for a few seconds until lightly browned.

5. Pour in the yoghurt and flour mixture and half the water. Bring to the boil, stirring.

6. Add the fried pakoras and remaining water. Bring to the boil, reduce the heat to medium-low then simmer for a further 25 minutes or until the required consistency has been obtained. Indians like to eat kadhi as runny as a soup with plain rice.

7. While the kadhi is cooking, prepare the tarka. Heat the ghee in a heavy-based pan and fry the mustard seeds until they start crackling. Add the onion and fry until golden brown.

8. Turn off the heat and stir in the garam masala, coriander and chilli. Pour the tarka on the kadhi before serving hot with plain rice, pickle or chutney and stuffed aubergine.

STUFFED MARROW

Serves 4

ingredients

	Metric	Imperial	American
Small marrow (squash), peeled	500 g	18 oz	18 oz
Oil or ghee	120 ml	4 fl oz	½ cup
Mustard seeds	5 ml	1 tsp	1 tsp
MARINADE			
Canned tomatoes	225 g	8 oz	½ lb
Natural yoghurt	150 ml	¼ pt	⅔ cup
Large garlic cloves, crushed	3	3	3
Fresh ginger root, chopped	1 cm	½ in	½ in
Medium onion, coarsely chopped	1	1	1
Garam masala	5 ml	1 tsp	1 tsp
Ground roasted cumin	5 ml	1 tsp	1 tsp
Ground red chilli	2.5 ml	½ tsp	½ tsp
Ground turmeric	2.5 ml	½ tsp	½ tsp
Salt to taste			
FILLING			
Ghee	30 ml	2 tbsp	2 tbsp
Desiccated coconut	50 g	2 oz	½ cup
Khoya	150 g	5 oz	5 oz
Raisins	100 g	4 oz	4 oz
Cashew nuts, halved lengthways	50 g	2 oz	½ cup
Almonds, blanched and halved lengthways	50 g	2 oz	½ cup
Sugar	15 ml	1 tbsp	1 tbsp
Ground cardamom	2.5 ml	½ tsp	½ tsp

method

1. Prick the marrow all over with a fork. Slit lengthways and scoop out all the seeds.

2. Blend all the marinade ingredients to a smooth paste in a blender or food processor. Rub over the marrow and leave to marinate for 4 hours.

3. For the filling, heat the ghee in a heavy-based pan and gently fry the coconut over a medium heat until lightly browned. Mix in the remaining filling ingredients and cook for a further 3 minutes.

4. Lift the marrow from the marinade. Heat the oil or ghee in a heavy-based pan and fry the mustard seeds until they start crackling. Add the marrow and fry for 2 minutes.

5. Pour in the remaining marinade carefully then cover with a lid as the mixture tends to spit. Cook for 25 minutes or until all the liquid has been absorbed and the marrow is tender, stirring occasionally.

6. Remove the lid and cook until the oil or ghee appears on the surface of the mixture.

7. Lift the marrow from the sauce and place it on a serving dish. Open the marrow and arrange the halves flat on the dish. Spoon the filling on top and pour the sauce around. Serve hot with puri, pulao, rayta and dal.

MUSHROOM CURRY

Serves 4

ingredients

	Metric	Imperial	American
Oil or ghee	60 ml	4 tbsp	4 tbsp
Cumin seeds	5 ml	1 tsp	1 tsp
Sesame seeds	2.5 ml	½ tsp	½ tsp
Large garlic cloves, crushed	2	2	2
Fresh ginger root, finely chopped	2.5 cm	1 in	1 in
Medium onion, finely chopped	1	1	1
Mushrooms, cut into 2.5 cm/1 in pieces	250 g	9 oz	9 oz
Garam masala	5 ml	1 tsp	1 tsp
Ground coriander	5 ml	1 tsp	1 tsp
Ground roasted cumin	5 ml	1 tsp	1 tsp
Ground red chilli	2.5 ml	½ tsp	½ tsp
Ground turmeric	2.5 ml	½ tsp	½ tsp
Ground mace	1.5 ml	¼ tsp	¼ tsp
Ground nutmeg	1.5 ml	¼ tsp	¼ tsp
Salt to taste			
Canned tomatoes	250 g	9 oz	9 oz
Frozen peas, thawed	250 g	9 oz	9 oz
Almonds, blanched and halved lengthways	50 g	2 oz	½ cup
Raisins	50 g	2 oz	⅔ cup
GARNISH			
Garam masala	1.5 ml	¼ tsp	¼ tsp
Chopped fresh coriander	15 ml	1 tbsp	1 tbsp
Small green chilli, chopped	1	1	1

26

method

1. Heat the oil in a heavy-based pan and fry the cumin and sesame seeds over a medium heat until lightly browned. Add the garlic, ginger and onion and fry gently until golden brown.

2. Stir in the mushrooms and fry for 2 minutes.

3. Stir in the garam masala, coriander, cumin, chilli, turmeric, mace, nutmeg and salt. Stir in the tomatoes, cover and cook over a medium-low heat for 10 minutes, stirring occasionally.

4. Remove the lid and cook until all the liquid has been absorbed and the oil appears on the surface of the mixture.

5. Stir in the peas, almonds and raisins and cook for a few minutes until the peas are tender. Increase the heat to allow any excess liquid to evaporate.

6. Sprinkle over the garnish ingredients and serve hot with puri, dal, rice and rayta.

INDIAN CHEESE CURRY

Serves 4

ingredients

	Metric	Imperial	American
Quantities Paneer (see page 95)	2	2	2
Oil for deep-frying			
Ghee or oil	60 ml	4 tbsp	4 tbsp
Cumin seeds	5 ml	1 tsp	1 tsp
Small onion, finely chopped	1	1	1
Cloves	4	4	4
Peppercorns	4	4	4
Bay leaves	2	2	2
Black cardamom pod	1	1	1
Large garlic cloves	3	3	3
Fresh ginger root	2.5 cm	1 in	1 in
Medium onion, cut into chunks	1	1	1
Water	45 ml	3 tbsp	3 tbsp
Ground coriander	7.5 ml	1½ tsp	1½ tsp
Ground red chilli	2.5 ml	½ tsp	½ tsp
Ground turmeric	2.5 ml	½ tsp	½ tsp
Canned tomatoes	225 g	8 oz	½ lb
Salt to taste			
Whey water (from paneer)	600 ml	1 pt	2½ cups
Frozen peas, thawed	500 g	18 oz	18 oz
GARNISH			
Garam masala	2.5 ml	½ tsp	½ tsp
Chopped fresh coriander	15 ml	1 tbsp	1 tbsp
Small green chilli, chopped	1	1	1

28

method

1. Chop the paneer into 1 cm/½ in cubes and fry in the oil until lightly browned. Remove with a slotted spoon and set aside.

2. Heat the ghee or oil in a heavy-based pan and fry the cumin seeds until lightly browned. Add the onion, cloves, peppercorns, bay leaves and cardamom and fry until golden brown.

3. Blend the garlic, ginger, onion and water to a smooth paste in a blender or food processor. Stir into the pan and fry for a few minutes until golden brown.

4. Add the coriander, chilli, turmeric, tomatoes and salt and cook over a medium heat until all the liquid has been absorbed.

5. Add 60 ml/4 tbsp of whey water to the pan and fry until all the water has been absorbed and the ghee appears on the surface of the mixture.

6. Add the remaining whey water and the fried paneer and simmer for 10 minutes.

(29)

7. Add the peas and simmer for a further 5 minutes until the peas are cooked and the paneer is soft and spongy.

8. Sprinkle over the garnish ingredients and serve hot with puri, pulao and a cauliflower dish.

STUFFED GREEN PEPPER

Serves 4

ingredients

	Metric	Imperial	American
FILLING			
Oil	45 ml	3 tbsp	3 tbsp
Mustard seeds	5 ml	1 tsp	1 tsp
Cumin seeds	5 ml	1 tsp	1 tsp
Potato, boiled and diced	1 kg	2 lb	2 lb
Ground coriander	30 ml	2 tbsp	3 tbsp
Ground roasted cumin	5 ml	1 tsp	1 tsp
Ground red chilli	2.5 ml	½ tsp	½ tsp
Ground turmeric	2.5 ml	½ tsp	½ tsp
Salt to taste			
Raisins	100 g	4 oz	⅔ cup
Lemon juice	30 ml	2 tbsp	2 tbsp
Sugar	10 ml	2 tsp	2 tsp
Garam masala	2.5 ml	½ tsp	½ tsp
Chopped fresh coriander	15 ml	1 tbsp	1 tbsp
Small green chilli, chopped	1	1	1
Small green peppers	500 g	18 oz	18 oz
SAUCE			
Oil	60 ml	4 tbsp	4 tbsp
Mustard seeds	2.5 ml	½ tsp	½ tsp
Small onion, finely chopped	1	1	1
Large onion, cut into large pieces	1	1	1
Large garlic cloves	3	3	3
Fresh ginger root	1 cm	½ in	½ in
Ground coriander	10 ml	2 tsp	2 tsp
Garam masala	2.5 ml	½ tsp	½ tsp
Ground red chilli	2.5 ml	½ tsp	½ tsp

Ground turmeric	2.5 ml	½ tsp	½ tsp
Canned tomatoes	400 g	14 oz	14 oz
Salt to taste			
Tamarind pulp (see page 94)	30 ml	2 tbsp	2 tbsp
GARNISH			
Garam masala	2.5 ml	½ tsp	½ tsp
Chopped fresh coriander	15 ml	1 tbsp	1 tbsp
Small green chilli, chopped	1	1	1

method

1. Heat the oil in a heavy–based pan and fry the mustard seeds until they start crackling. Add the cumin seeds and diced potatoes and fry over a medium heat for 2-3 minutes.

2. Stir in the coriander, cumin, chilli, turmeric and salt and fry for a further 2-3 minutes.

31

3. Add the raisins, lemon juice, sugar, garam masala, coriander and chilli and cook for 1 minute. Remove from the heat.

4. Slice the top off the peppers and scoop out the seeds. Fill the peppers with the potato stuffing and put back the lids.

5. Stand a trivet in a large pan and fill with water to come half way up the trivet. Place the peppers on the trivet, bring the water to the boil then reduce the heat to low, cover and steam for 20 minutes, turning once while cooking.

6. Meanwhile, make the sauce. Heat the oil in a large frying pan (skillet) and fry the mustard seeds until they start crackling. Add the chopped onion and fry until golden brown.

7. Blend the onion, garlic and ginger to a smooth paste in a blender or food processor. Stir into the pan and fry until golden brown.

8 Add the coriander, garam masala, chilli, turmeric, tomatoes and salt and cook until the oil appears on the top of the mixture.

9. Stir in the tamarind pulp and cook until all the liquid has been absorbed.

10. Reduce the heat to low and add the cooked stuffed peppers to the pan. Cook for 5 minutes over a low heat, basting the peppers with the sauce.

11. Transfer to a serving dish, sprinkle with the garnish ingredients and serve hot with lentils, rice and onion paratha.

GREEN PEPPER AND POTATO

Serves 2

ingredients

	Metric	Imperial	American
Oil	*60 ml*	*4 tbsp*	*4 tbsp*
Small pinch of asafoetida			
Mustard seeds	*2.5 ml*	*½ tsp*	*½ tsp*
Onion seeds	*2.5 ml*	*½ tsp*	*½ tsp*
Potatoes, cut into 2.5 cm/1 in pieces	*250 g*	*9 oz*	*9 oz*
Green pepper, cut into 2.5 cm/ 1 in pieces			
Ground coriander	*5 ml*	*1 tsp*	*1 tsp*
Ground roasted cumin	*5 ml*	*1 tsp*	*1 tsp*
Garam masala	*2.5 ml*	*½ tsp*	*½ tsp*
Ground red chilli	*2.5 ml*	*½ tsp*	*½ tsp*
Ground turmeric	*2.5 ml*	*½ tsp*	*½ tsp*
Salt to taste			
GARNISH			
Garam masala	*1.5 ml*	*¼ tsp*	*¼ tsp*
Chopped fresh coriander	*15 ml*	*1 tbsp*	*1 tbsp*

method

1. Heat the oil in a heavy-based pan and fry the asafoetida, mustard and onion seeds over a medium heat until they start crackling. Add the potato pieces and fry until lightly browned. Add the pepper and cook for 1 minute.

2. Stir in the spices and salt, reduce the heat to low and cook for about 10 minutes until tender, stirring occasionally.

3. Sprinkle with the garnish ingredients and serve hot with dal, rice, puri or chapati and a kofta dish.

POTATO CURRY

Serves 4

ingredients

(33)

	Metric	Imperial	American
Potatoes	500 g	18 oz	18 oz
Oil or ghee	60 ml	4 tbsp	4 tbsp
Mustard seeds	2.5 ml	½ tsp	½ tsp
Cumin seeds	2.5 ml	½ tsp	½ tsp
Ground coriander	5 ml	1 tsp	1 tsp
Ground roasted cumin	5 ml	1 tsp	1 tsp
Garam masala	2.5 ml	½ tsp	½ tsp
Ground red chilli	2.5 ml	½ tsp	½ tsp
Ground turmeric	2.5 ml	½ tsp	½ tsp
Salt to taste			
Canned tomatoes	400 g	14 oz	14 oz
Water	150 ml	¼ pt	⅔ cup
Lemon juice	30 ml	2 tbsp	2 tbsp
GARNISH			
Garam masala	1.5 ml	¼ tsp	¼ tsp
Chopped fresh coriander	15 ml	1 tbsp	1 tbsp
Small green chilli, chopped	1	1	1

method

1. Boil the potatoes in their skins then drain, peel and cut into 5 mm/¼ in pieces.

2. Heat the oil in a heavy-based pan and fry the mustard seeds over a medium heat until they start crackling. Add the cumin seeds and fry for a few seconds until lightly browned.

3. Stir in the potato pieces and fry until lightly browned.

4. Stir in the coriander, cumin, garam masala, chilli, turmeric and salt. Stir in the tomatoes and cook until the water has been absorbed.

5. Pour in the water, bring to the boil then reduce the heat to low and simmer for 2 minutes.

6. Add the lemon juice. Sprinkle with the garnish ingredients and serve hot with puri, lasi and pickle at breakfast.

POTATO AND PEAS

ingredients

Serves 4

	Metric	Imperial	American
Potatoes, cut into 2.5 cm/1 in pieces	250 g	9 oz	9 oz
Oil for deep-frying			
Oil or ghee	75 ml	5 tbsp	5 tbsp
Small onion, finely chopped	1	1	1
Large garlic cloves	3	3	3
Medium onion, coarsely chopped	1	1	1
Fresh ginger root	1 cm	½ in	½ in
Water	175 ml	6 fl oz	⅔ cup
Ground coriander	10 ml	2 tsp	2 tsp
Ground roasted cumin	5 ml	1 tsp	1 tsp
Garam masala	2.5 ml	½ tsp	½ tsp
Ground red chilli	2.5 ml	½ tsp	½ tsp

Ground turmeric	*2.5 ml*	*½ tsp*	*½ tsp*
Salt to taste			
Canned tomatoes	*225 g*	*8 oz*	*½ lb*
Natural yoghurt	*150 ml*	*¼ pt*	*⅔ cup*
Frozen peas, thawed	*450 g*	*1 lb*	*1 lb*
GARNISH			
Garam masala	*2.5 ml*	*½ tsp*	*½ tsp*
Chopped fresh			
coriander	*15 ml*	*1 tbsp*	*1 tbsp*
Small green chilli,			
chopped	*1*	*1*	*1*

method

1. Deep-fry the potato in the oil over a medium heat until golden brown.

2. Meanwhile, heat the oil or ghee in a heavy-based pan and gently fry the small onion until golden.

3. Blend the garlic, medium onion, ginger and 30 ml/2 tbsp of water to a smooth paste in a blender or food processor. Add it to the pan and fry for a further few minutes until golden brown.

4. Stir in the coriander, cumin, garam masala, chilli, turmeric and salt. Stir in the tomatoes. Simmer until all the liquid has been absorbed and oil appears on the top of the mixture.

5. Stir in the yoghurt and simmer until the liquid has been absorbed.

6. Stir in the remaining water with the potatoes and peas, cover and simmer for 3 minutes. (If you use fresh peas, add them with an extra 150 ml/¼ pt/⅔ cup of water and simmer until tender before adding the potatoes.)

7. Sprinkle over the garnish ingredients and serve hot with rice, dal or rayta.

VEGETABLE SAMOSAS

Makes 16

ingredients

	Metric	Imperial	American
Plain flour	200 g	7 oz	1⅔ cups
Lemon juice	5 ml	1 tsp	1 tsp
Small pinch of salt			
Lukewarm water	75 ml	5 tbsp	5 tbsp
FILLING			
Oil	45 ml	3 tbsp	3 tbsp
Cumin seeds	5 ml	1 tsp	1 tsp
Potatoes, boiled in their skins then chopped	500 g	18 oz	18 oz
Garam masala	5 ml	1 tsp	1 tsp
Ground roasted cumin	5 ml	1 tsp	1 tsp
Ground ginger	2.5 ml	½ tsp	½ tsp
Ground red chilli	2.5 ml	½ tsp	½ tsp
Ground turmeric	2.5 ml	½ tsp	½ tsp
Salt to taste			
Frozen peas, thawed	225 g	8 oz	½ lb
Lemon juice	30 ml	2 tbsp	2 tbsp
Sugar	15 ml	1 tbsp	1 tbsp
Chopped fresh coriander	60 ml	4 tbsp	4 tbsp
Small green chilli, chopped	1	1	1
BATTER			
Plain (all-purpose) flour	15 ml	1 tbsp	1 tbsp
Water	15-30 ml	1-2 tbsp	1-2 tbsp
Oil for frying			

method

1. Sift 150 g/5 oz/1¼ cups of flour into a bowl and mix in the lemon juice and salt. Work in the water to form a dough then knead for 5 minutes until the dough is springy and satiny. Cover and set aside for 30 minutes.

2. To make the filling, heat the oil in a heavy–based pan and fry the cumin seeds until lightly browned. Add the potato pieces and fry for 10 minutes until light golden brown.

3. Stir in the garam masala, cumin, ginger, chilli, turmeric and salt. Stir in the peas and simmer for about 3 minutes until tender.

4. Stir in the lemon juice and sugar and cook for 2 minutes. Remove from the heat and stir in the coriander and chilli. Leave to cool then divide into 16 equal portions.

5. Make a runny batter with the flour and a little water and set aside.

6. Divide the dough into 8 equal portions and roll each one into a ball. Dust with flour then roll into circles. Place a circle on a floured board, smear the top with oil, sprinkle with flour and top with another circle. Repeat this until you have 4 circles one on top of each other. Sprinkle with flour then roll out thinly.

7. Heat a flat frying pan (skillet) over a medium heat. Reduce the heat to low and place the rolled circles in it. Fry for 10-20 seconds until dry, turn over and remove the first layer. Immediately turn over again and remove the second layer and continue until both sides of all the layers are cooked. Place on a cooling tray and cover with a teacloth. Cook the remaining dough.

8. Cut the rounds in half and overlap the flat sides to form a cone shape. Brush the edges with the batter and seal them firmly.

9. Fill the cones with the potato mixture, brush the edges with batter and seal firmly.

10. Heat the oil in a deep pan over a medium heat. Gently slip 5 or 6 samosas into the hot oil, reduce the heat to medium-low and fry gently until crispy light golden brown on all sides.

SWEET AND SOUR VEGETABLES

Serves 6

ingredients

	Metric	Imperial	American
BATTER			
Gram flour	100 g	4 oz	1 cup
Oil	15 ml	1 tbsp	1 tbsp
Chopped fresh coriander	15 ml	1 tbsp	1 tbsp
Ajowain	5 ml	1 tsp	1 tsp
Garam masala	2.5 ml	½ tsp	½ tsp
Ground red chilli	2.5 ml	½ tsp	½ tsp
Salt to taste			
Warm water	150 ml	¼ pt	⅔ cup
Oil for deep–frying			
Mixed vegetables (cauliflower, carrots, green pepper, aubergine (eggplant) etc.), cut into 4 cm/ 1½ in pieces	675 g	1½ lb	1½ lb
SAUCE			
Oil or ghee	75 ml	5 tbsp	5 tbsp
Small onion, finely chopped	1	1	1
Large garlic cloves, crushed	4	4	4
Fresh ginger root, coarsely chopped	2.5 cm	1 in	1 in
Medium onion, coarsely chopped	1	1	1
Ground coriander	10 ml	2 tsp	2 tsp
Garam masala	5 ml	1 tsp	1 tsp
Ground roasted cumin	5 ml	1 tsp	1 tsp
Ground red chilli	2.5 ml	½ tsp	½ tsp

Ground turmeric	2.5 ml	½ tsp	½ tsp
Ground mace	1.5 ml	¼ tsp	¼ tsp
Ground nutmeg	1.5 ml	¼ tsp	¼ tsp
Salt to taste			
Canned tomatoes	225 g	8 oz	½ lb
Vinegar	60 ml	4 tbsp	4 tbsp
Clear honey	15 ml	1 tbsp	1 tbsp
Water	200 ml	7 fl oz	scant 1 cup
GARNISH			
Garam masala	2.5 ml	½ tsp	½ tsp
Chopped fresh			
coriander	15 ml	1 tbsp	1 tbsp

method

1. Beat together all the batter ingredients until smooth. Dip the vegetables into the batter and deep-fry in batches in hot oil until golden brown. Arrange on a serving dish and set aside.

2. Heat the oil in a heavy-based pan and fry the small onion until golden brown.

3. Blend the garlic, ginger and onion to a smooth paste in a blender or food processor. Stir into the pan with the spices and tomatoes and cook until all the liquid has been absorbed and the oil appears on the surface of the mixture.

4. Pour in the vinegar and cook until all the liquid is absorbed.

5. Add the honey and cook for a further 2 minutes.

6. Add the water and bring to the boil. Simmer over a low heat for 2 minutes.

7. Pour the hot sauce over the vegetables, sprinkle with the garnish ingredients and serve hot with rice, puri, rayta and chutney.

VEGETARIAN KEEMA

ingredients

	Metric	Imperial	American
Ghee	60 ml	4 tbsp	4 tbsp
Bay leaves	2	2	2
Large garlic cloves, crushed	2	2	2
Fresh ginger root, finely chopped	1 cm	½ in	½ in
Medium onion, finely chopped	1	1	1
Garam masala	5 ml	1 tsp	1 tsp
Ground roasted cumin	5 ml	1 tsp	1 tsp
Ground coriander	5 ml	1 tsp	1 tsp
Ground red chilli	2.5 ml	½ tsp	½ tsp
Ground turmeric	2.5 ml	½ tsp	½ tsp
Salt to taste			
Canned tomatoes	225 g	8 oz	½ lb
Khoya (see page 94), broken into pieces	150 g	5 oz	5 oz
Raisins	100 g	4 oz	⅔ cup
Cashew nuts, halved lengthways	50 g	2 oz	½ cup
Ground green cardamom	1.5 ml	¼ tsp	¼ tsp
GARNISH			
Garam masala	1.5 ml	¼ tsp	¼ tsp
Chopped fresh coriander	15 ml	1 tbsp	1 tbsp
Small green chilli, chopped	1	1	1

method

1. Heat the ghee in a heavy-based pan and fry the bay leaves, garlic, ginger and onion over a medium heat until golden brown.

2. Stir in the garam masala, cumin, coriander, chilli, turmeric and salt. Stir in the tomatoes and fry for about 15 minutes until all the liquid has been absorbed and the ghee appears on the surface of the mixture.

3. Mix in the khoya, raisins and nuts, reduce the heat to low and cook for a further 2 minutes.

4. Sprinkle over the garnish ingredients and serve hot with pulao, rayta and a kofta dish.

VEGETABLE BIRYANI

Serves 4

ingredients

	Metric	Imperial	American
Oil or ghee	60 ml	4 tbsp	4 tbsp
Cumin seeds	2.5 ml	½ tsp	½ tsp
Large garlic cloves, crushed	2	2	2
Fresh ginger root, finely chopped	1 cm	½ in	½ in
Medium onion, finely chopped	1	1	1
Desiccated coconut	60 ml	4 tbsp	4 tbsp
Garam masala	5 ml	1 tsp	1 tsp
Ground coriander	5 ml	1 tsp	1 tsp
Ground roasted cumin	5 ml	1 tsp	1 tsp
Ground red chilli	2.5 ml	½ tsp	½ tsp
Ground turmeric	2.5 ml	½ tsp	½ tsp
Salt to taste			
Canned tomatoes	400 g	14 oz	14 oz
Frozen sweetcorn, thawed	250 g	9 oz	9 oz
Quantity Paneer (see page 94), cut into 1 cm/½ in pieces	1	1	1
Chopped fresh coriander	30 ml	2 tbsp	2 tbsp
Lemon juice	30 ml	2 tbsp	2 tbsp
Chopped fresh mint	15 ml	1 tbsp	1 tbsp
RICE			
Ghee	90 ml	6 tbsp	6 tbsp
Cumin seeds	5 ml	1 tsp	1 tsp
Medium onion, thinly sliced	1	1	1
Cloves	4	4	4

42

Peppercorns	4	4	4
Cinnamon stick	2.5 cm	1 in	1 in
Bay leaves	2	2	2
Black cardamom pod	1	1	1
Patna or basmati rice, washed and drained	225 g	8 oz	1 cup
Garam masala	5 ml	1 tsp	1 tsp
Ground roasted cumin	5 ml	1 tsp	1 tsp
Salt to taste			
Raisins	100 g	4 oz	⅔ cup
Almonds, blanched and halved lengthways	50 g	2 oz	½ cup
Cashew nuts, halved lengthways	50 g	2 oz	½ cup
Water	500 ml	17 fl oz	2¼ cups
TO FINISH			
Ground saffron	2.5 ml	½ tsp	½ tsp
Warm milk	45 ml	3 tbsp	3 tbsp

method

1. Heat the oil or ghee in a heavy-based pan and fry the cumin seeds until lightly browned. Add the garlic, ginger and onion and fry until golden brown.

2. Stir in the coconut and fry for 2 minutes.

3. Stir in the garam masala, coriander, cumin, chilli, turmeric and salt. Stir in the tomatoes, sweetcorn and paneer. Cook for about 20 minutes until all the liquid has been absorbed.

4. Stir in the coriander, lemon juice and mint. Remove from the heat and set aside.

5. Meanwhile, cook the rice. Heat the ghee in a heavy–based pan and fry the cumin seeds until lightly browned. Add the onion, cloves, peppercorns, cinnamon, bay leaves and cardamom and fry until golden brown.

6. Mix in the rice and fry for 2 minutes. Stir in the garam masala, cumin and salt. Stir in the raisins, nuts and water and bring to the boil. Reduce the heat to low, cover and cook for 10 minutes.

7. Dissolve the saffron in the warm milk.

8. To assemble the dish, layer the vegetables and rice in a heavy-based pan and pour over the saffron milk. Cover and cook over a low heat for 5 minutes.

9. Before serving, place a serving dish on the saucepan and carefully turn them over. Tap a little with a spoon on the pan and gently lift it off, leaving the biryani in the serving dish. Serve hot with rayta, salad, and potatoes and peas.

VEGETABLE SCOTCH

(44)

Makes 12

ingredients

	Metric	Imperial	American
Mixed vegetables	500 g	18 oz	18 oz
Oil	45 ml	3 tbsp	3 tbsp
Medium onion, finely chopped	1	1	1
Fresh ginger root, finely chopped	2.5 cm	1 in	1 in
Garam masala	5 ml	1 tsp	1 tsp
Ground roasted cumin	5 ml	1 tsp	1 tsp
Ground red chilli	2.5 ml	½ tsp	½ tsp
Salt to taste			
Lemon juice	30 ml	2 tsp	2 tbsp
Chopped fresh coriander	30 ml	2 tbsp	2 tbsp
Small green chilli, chopped	1	1	1

BATTER			
Rice flour	*50 g*	*2 oz*	*½ cup*
Warm water	*75 ml*	*5 tbsp*	*5 tbsp*
Quantity Paneer (see page 95), cut into 12	*1*	*1*	*1*
Oil for deep-frying			

method

1. Boil the vegetables in water until tender then drain.

2. Heat the oil in a heavy-based pan and fry the onion and ginger until lightly browned.

3. Add the cooked vegetables and fry until lightly browned.

4. Stir in the garam masala, cumin, chilli and salt, mix thoroughly and form into a thick paste. Stir in the lemon juice, coriander and chilli.

(45)

5. Divide into 12 equal portions. Take one portion at a time and flatten it. Place a piece of paneer on top, bring the edges of the vegetable paste over to cover it and shape it into a rectangle.

6. Mix together the batter ingredients to a runny batter and season with salt to taste.

7. Heat the oil in a deep pan. Dip a vegetable scotch in the batter and add it to the hot oil. Fry 5 or 6 at a time until golden brown. Serve hot with chutney and barfi at tea.

MIXED VEGETABLE KORMA

Serves 4

ingredients

	Metric	Imperial	American
Oil	75 ml	5 tbsp	5 tbsp
Fenugreek seeds	5 ml	1 tsp	1 tsp
Large garlic cloves, crushed	3	3	3
Fresh ginger root, finely chopped	2.5 cm	1 in	1 in
Medium onion, finely chopped	1	1	1
Desiccated coconut, ground	90 ml	6 tbsp	6 tbsp
Garam masala	5 ml	1 tsp	1 tsp
Ground coriander	5 ml	1 tsp	1 tsp
Ground roasted cumin	5 ml	1 tsp	1 tsp
Ground red chilli	2.5 ml	½ tsp	½ tsp
Ground turmeric	2.5 ml	½ tsp	½ tsp
Canned tomatoes	400 g	14 oz	14 oz
Cauliflower, cut into florets	500 g	18 oz	18 oz
Small carrots, cut into 4 cm/1½ in pieces	6	6	6
Water	600 ml	1 pt	2½ cups
Medium aubergine (eggplant), cut into 1 cm/½ in pieces	1	1	1
Medium pepper, cut into 1 cm/½ in pieces	1	1	1
Medium potato, cut into 1 cm/½ in pieces	1	1	1
Tamarind pulp (see page 94)	10 ml	2 tsp	2 tsp

46

GARNISH			
Garam masala	1.5 ml	¼ tsp	¼ tsp
Chopped fresh coriander	15 ml	1 tbsp	1 tbsp
Small green chilli, chopped	1	1	1

method

1. Heat the oil in a heavy-based pan and fry the fenugreek seeds until lightly browned. Add the garlic, ginger and onion and fry until golden brown.

2. Stir in the coconut, garam masala, coriander, cumin, chilli and turmeric. Stir in the tomatoes and cook until all the liquid has been absorbed and the oil appears on the surface of the mixture.

3. Add the cauliflower and carrots and 200 ml/7 fl oz/scant 1 cup of water and bring to the boil. Reduce the heat to medium-low and cook for 15 minutes.

4. Add the remaining vegetables and water and the tamarind pulp and cook for a further 30 minutes until the vegetables are tender.

5. Sprinkle over the garnish ingredients and serve hot with idli or puri, yoghurt, rice and dal.

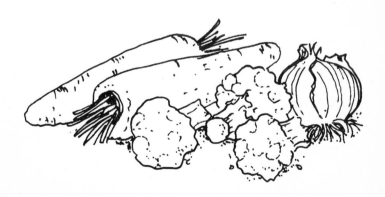

MIXED VEGETABLES AND POTATO

Serves 4

ingredients

	Metric	Imperial	American
Oil for frying			
Medium potatoes, peeled and quartered	250 g	9 oz	9 oz
Oil or ghee	75 ml	5 tbsp	5 tbsp
Mustard seeds	5 ml	1 tsp	1 tsp
Bay leaves	2	2	2
Small onion, finely chopped	1	1	1
Medium onion, coarsely chopped	1	1	1
Large garlic cloves	2	2	2
Fresh ginger root	1 cm	½ in	½ in
Garam masala	5 ml	1 tsp	1 tsp
Ground coriander	5 ml	1 tsp	1 tsp
Ground roasted cumin	5 ml	1 tsp	1 tsp
Ground red chilli	2.5 ml	½ tsp	½ tsp
Ground turmeric	2.5 ml	½ tsp	½ tsp
Ground mace	1.5 ml	¼ tsp	¼ tsp
Ground nutmeg	1.5 ml	¼ tsp	¼ tsp
Salt to taste			
Canned tomatoes	400 g	14 oz	14 oz
Water	50 ml	2 fl oz	3½ tbsp
Frozen mixed vegetables, thawed	500 g	18 oz	18 oz
GARNISH			
Garam masala	2.5 ml	½ tsp	½ tsp
Chopped fresh coriander	15 ml	1 tbsp	1 tbsp
Small green chilli, chopped	1	1	1

method

1. Heat the frying oil and fry the potatoes over a medium heat until golden brown. Drain well.

2. Meanwhile, heat the oil or ghee and fry the mustard seeds over a medium heat until they start crackling. Add the bay leaves and chopped onion and fry until golden brown.

3. Blend the onion, garlic and ginger to a smooth paste in a blender or food processor. Stir into the pan and fry for a few minutes until golden brown.

4. Stir in the garam masala, coriander, cumin, chilli, turmeric, mace, nutmeg and salt. Stir in the tomatoes and cook until all the liquid has been absorbed and the oil appears on the surface of the mixture. Add the water and cook until the liquid is absorbed.

5. Stir in the vegetables and potatoes. Cover and cook over a medium heat for about 15 minutes until the vegetables are tender.

6. Sprinkle with the garnish ingredients and serve hot with onion paratha or puri, rice, dal and rayta.

▼

Pulses

SABAT MOONG DAL

Serves 4 - 6

ingredients

	Metric	Imperial	American
Sabat moong dal, soaked for 1 hour	250 g	9 oz	1½ cups
Water	1.5 l	2½ pts	6 cups
Large pinch of ground turmeric			
Salt to taste			
TARKA			
Oil or ghee	45 ml	3 tbsp	3 tbsp
Cumin seeds	5 ml	1 tsp	1 tsp
Medium onion, finely chopped	1	1	1
Fresh ginger root, finely chopped	1 cm	½ in	½ in
Ground red chilli	2.5 ml	½ tsp	½ tsp
Large pinch of ground turmeric			
Canned tomatoes	225 g	8 oz	½ lb
GARNISH			
Chopped fresh coriander	15 ml	1 tbsp	1 tbsp
Garam masala	2.5 ml	½ tsp	½ tsp
Small green chilli, chopped	1	1	1

method

1. Place the dal, water, turmeric and salt in a pan, bring to the boil and skim off any scum. Reduce the heat, cover and simmer for 50 minutes over a medium heat until tender.

2. Meanwhile, heat the oil or ghee in a heavy-based pan and fry the cumin seeds until lightly browned. Add the onion and ginger and fry until golden brown.

3. Add the chilli, turmeric and tomatoes and cook for about 40 minutes until all the water has been absorbed and the ghee appears on the top of the mixture.

4. Stir in the cooked dal and simmer for a further 10 minutes.

5. Sprinkle with the garnish ingredients and serve hot with rice, chapati, Indian cheese curry, cauliflower and yoghurt.

51

CHICK PEAS IN SAUCE

Serves 4

ingredients

	Metric	Imperial	American
Chick peas (garbanzo beans), soaked overnight	250 g	9 oz	9 oz
Bicarbonate of soda (baking soda)	2.5 ml	½ tsp	½ tsp
Water	1.75 l	3 pts	7½ cups
Salt to taste			
Ghee or oil	90 ml	6 tbsp	6 tbsp
Small onion, finely chopped	1	1	1
Cloves	4	4	4
Peppercorns	4	4	4
Bay leaves	2	2	2
Cinnamon stick	1 cm	½ in	½ in
Black cardamom pod	1	1	1
Large garlic cloves	4	4	4
Fresh ginger root, coarsely chopped	2.5 cm	1 in	1 in
Large onion, coarsely chopped	1	1	1
Water	45 ml	3 tbsp	3 tbsp
Ground coriander	5 ml	1 tsp	1 tsp
Ground roasted cumin	5 ml	1 tsp	1 tsp
Garam masala	2.5 ml	½ tsp	½ tsp
Ground red chilli	2.5 ml	½ tsp	½ tsp
Ground turmeric	2.5 ml	½ tsp	½ tsp
Ground mace	1.5 ml	¼ tsp	¼ tsp
Ground nutmeg	1.5 ml	¼ tsp	¼ tsp
Salt to taste			
Canned tomatoes	400 g	14 oz	14 oz
Potatoes, boiled and diced	225 g	8 oz	8 oz

GARNISH			
Garam masala	1.5 ml	¼ tsp	¼ tsp
Chopped fresh coriander	15 ml	1 tbsp	1 tbsp
Small green chilli, chopped	1	1	1

method

1. Place the chick peas in a large pan with the bicarbonate of soda, water and salt. Bring to the boil, skim off any scum, cover and simmer gently for 1 hour until the chick peas are tender.

2. Meanwhile, heat the ghee or oil in a heavy–based pan and fry the onion, cloves, peppercorns, bay leaves, cinnamon and cardamom until golden brown.

3. Blend the garlic, ginger, onion and water to a smooth paste in a blender or food processor. Add it to the pan and fry for a few minutes until golden brown.

4. Stir in the coriander, cumin, garam masala, chilli, turmeric, mace, nutmeg and salt to taste. Stir in the tomatoes and simmer until all the liquid has been absorbed and the ghee appears on the surface of the mixture.

5. Drain the chick peas then mix them into the sauce. Simmer until the chick peas are thoroughly tender and have absorbed the flavours of the sauce.

6. Stir in the potato and cook for 5 minutes.

7. Sprinkle over the garnish ingredients and serve hot with plain rice, chapati, rayta and okra.

CHICK PEAS WITH TAMARIND

Serves 4

ingredients

	Metric	Imperial	American
Chick peas (garbanzo beans), soaked overnight	500 g	18 oz	18 oz
Gram dal, cleaned	50 g	2 oz	⅔ cup
Water	2.8 l	5 pts	12 cups
Bicarbonate of soda (baking soda)	2.5 ml	½ tsp	½ tsp
Salt to taste			
Oil or ghee	75 ml	5 tbsp	5 tbsp
Cumin seeds	5 ml	1 tsp	1 tsp
Large garlic cloves, crushed	3	3	3
Fresh ginger root, chopped	2.5 cm	1 in	1 in
Large onion, finely chopped	1	1	1
Ground coriander	10 ml	2 tsp	2 tsp
Ground roasted cumin	5 ml	1 tsp	1 tsp
Garam masala	5 ml	1 tsp	1 tsp
Ground turmeric	2.5 ml	½ tsp	½ tsp
Ground red chilli	2.5 ml	½ tsp	½ tsp
Canned tomatoes	400 g	14 oz	14 oz
Tamarind pulp (see page 94)	10 ml	2 tsp	2 tsp
GARNISH			
Chopped fresh coriander	30 ml	2 tbsp	2 tbsp
Small green chilli chopped	1	1	1
Garam masala	2.5 ml	½ tsp	½ tsp

54

method

1. Place the chick peas, gram dal, bicarbonate of soda, salt and water in a large pan. If you do not have a pan large enough, add the water gradually. Bring to the boil, skim off any scum and simmer over a medium heat for 1 hour 20 minutes until the chick peas are tender. Drain.

2. Meanwhile, heat the oil in a heavy-based pan and fry the cumin seeds until lightly browned. Add the garlic, ginger and onion and fry over a medium heat until golden brown.

3. Stir in the coriander, cumin, garam masala, turmeric and chilli. Stir in the tomatoes and cook until all the water has been absorbed and the oil appears on the top of the mixture.

4. Add the tamarind pulp and cook until all the liquid has been absorbed.

5. Stir in the cooked chick peas and simmer over a medium heat for a further 20 minutes until the mixture thickens.

6. Sprinkle with the garnish ingredients and serve hot with nan, tamarind chutney, potato curry and a chopped onion, cucumber and tomato salad.

DAL WITH COCONUT

Serves 4

ingredients

	Metric	Imperial	American
Gram dal, cleaned and soaked for 1 hour	250 g	9 oz	1½ cups
Ground turmeric	2.5 ml	½ tsp	½ tsp
Water	1.75 l	3 pts	7½ cups
Salt to taste			
TARKA			
Oil	45 ml	3 tbsp	3 tbsp
Cumin seeds	5 ml	1 tsp	1 tsp
Small onion, finely chopped	1	1	1
Fresh ginger root, finely chopped	1 cm	½ in	½ in
Bay leaves	2	2	2
Desiccated coconut	50 g	2 oz	½ cup
Garam masala	2.5 ml	½ tsp	½ tsp
Ground red chilli	2.5 ml	½ tsp	½ tsp
Ground turmeric	1.5 ml	¼ tsp	¼ tsp
Small green chilli, finely chopped	1	1	1
Tamarind pulp (see page 94)	5 ml	1 tsp	1 tsp
Sugar	25 g	1 oz	2 tbsp
GARNISH			
Chopped fresh coriander	15 ml	1 tbsp	1 tbsp
Garam masala	2.5 ml	½ tsp	½ tsp

method

1. Put the dal, turmeric, water and salt in a pan and bring to the boil. Skim off any scum, reduce the heat, cover and simmer over a medium heat for about 1 hour until tender.

2. Meanwhile, heat the oil in a heavy-based pan and fry the cumin seeds until lightly browned. Add the onion, ginger and bay leaves and fry until lightly browned.

3. Stir in the coconut and fry until golden brown.

4. Stir in the garam masala, chilli, turmeric and green chilli and tamarind pulp and bring to the boil.

5. Stir the tarka into the cooked lentils then simmer for a further 10 minutes.

6. Sprinkle over the garnish ingredients and serve hot with plain rice, okra and rayta.

57

SAMBAR

Serves 4

ingredients

	Metric	Imperial	American
SAMBAR MASALA			
Desiccated coconut	50 g	2 oz	½ cup
Oil	15 ml	1 tbsp	1 tbsp
Whole coriander	15 ml	1 tbsp	1 tbsp
Urud ki dhuki dal	10 ml	2 tsp	2 tsp
Gram dal	10 ml	2 tsp	2 tsp
Fenugreek seeds	5 ml	1 tsp	1 tsp
Whole dried red chilli	4	4	4
SAMBA			
Arhar dal, washed and drained	250 g	9 oz	1½ cups
Water	1.2 l	2 pts	5 cups
Ground turmeric	5 ml	1 tsp	1 tsp
Salt to taste			
Aubergine (eggplant) or okra, cut into 5 mm/¼ in thick pieces	250 g	9 oz	9 oz
Tamarind pulp (see page 94)	15 ml	1 tbsp	1 tbsp
TARKA			
Oil	90 ml	6 tbsp	6 tbsp
Large pinch of asafoetida			
Mustard seeds	5 ml	1 tsp	1 tsp
Curry leaves or bay leaves	3	3	3
Small onion, thinly sliced	3	3	3
Garam masala	5 ml	1 tsp	1 tsp
Canned tomatoes	400 g	14 oz	14 oz
Chopped fresh coriander	90 ml	6 tbsp	6 tbsp

method

1. Heat the oil in a frying pan (skillet) on a medium-low heat and roast all the sambar masala ingredients for about 5 minutes until light brown. Leave to cool then grind to a fine paste.

2. Place the dal, water, turmeric and salt in a large pan, bring to the boil and skim off any scum. Reduce the heat, cover and simmer for 30 minutes until the dal is tender.

3. Meanwhile, cook the aubergine in the tamarind pulp for 5 minutes.

4. Bring to the boil then add the sambar masala. Cook on a medium–low heat for 10 minutes or until the aubergine is tender.

5. Mix in the cooked dal.

6. Meanwhile, heat the oil and fry the asafoetida and mustard seeds until they start crackling. Add the onion and curry or bay leaves and onion and fry until golden brown.

7. Stir in the garam masala and tomatoes and cook until all the liquid has been absorbed and the oil appears on the surface of the mixture.

8. Add the coriander and mix in the cooked dal. Bring to the boil, reduce the heat then simmer for 5 minutes.

9. Serve hot with rice, rayta and cauliflower or potato.

URUD DAL

ingredients

	Metric	Imperial	American
Urud dal	350 g	12 oz	3 cups
Ground turmeric	2.5 ml	½ tsp	½ tsp
Water	900 ml	1½ pts	3⅘ cups
Salt to taste			
TARKA			
Ghee or oil	60 ml	4 tbsp	4 tbsp
Large pinch of asafoetida			
Large garlic cloves, crushed	3	3	3
Fresh ginger root, chopped	2.5 cm	1 in	1 in
Large onion, chopped	1	1	1
Ground roasted cumin	5 ml	1 tsp	1 tsp
Ground red chilli	2.5 ml	½ tsp	½ tsp
Ground turmeric	1.5 ml	¼ tsp	¼ tsp
Garam masala	2.5 ml	½ tsp	½ tsp
GARNISH			
Chopped fresh coriander	15 ml	1 tbsp	1 tbsp
Garam masala	2.5 ml	½ tsp	½ tsp
Small green chilli, chopped	1	1	1

method

1. Place the dal, turmeric, water and salt in a large pan, bring to the boil and skim off any scum. Reduce the heat, cover and simmer over a low heat for 45 minutes until the dal is tender. If any water is left, dry it off on a high heat but don't stir or the dal will become mushy.

2. Meanwhile, heat the ghee or oil in a heavy-based pan and fry the asafoetida, garlic, ginger and onion over a medium heat until golden brown.

3. Add the cumin, chilli, turmeric and garam masala and stir in the cooked dal.

4. Sprinkle with the garnish ingredients and serve hot with chapati, stuffed aubergine, potato curry and rayta.

61

MARROW WITH LENTILS

Serves 4

ingredients

	Metric	Imperial	American
Gram dal, washed and drained	250 g	9 oz	1½ cups
Ground turmeric	5 ml	1 tsp	1 tsp
Water	1.75 l	3 pts	7½ cups
Marrow (squash), peeled and cut into 1 cm/½ in pieces	250 g	9 oz	9 oz
Lemon juice	30 ml	2 tsp	2 tsp
TARKA			
Ghee	75 ml	5 tbsp	5 tbsp
Cumin seeds	5 ml	1 tsp	1 tsp
Large garlic cloves, crushed	2	2	2
Fresh ginger root, finely chopped	1 cm	½ in	½ in
Medium onion, finely chopped	1	1	1
Chopped fresh coriander	45 ml	3 tbsp	3 tbsp
Garam masala	5 ml	1 tsp	1 tsp
Ground red chilli	1.5 ml	½ tsp	½ tsp
Small green chilli, chopped	1	1	1

method

1. Place the dal in a heavy-based pan with the turmeric, salt and water. Bring to the boil and skim off any scum. Reduce the heat to medium-low, cover and cook for 25 minutes.

2. Add the marrow and cook for a further 25 minutes until the dal and vegetables are tender.

3. Stir in the lemon juice.

4. Meanwhile, heat the ghee in a heavy-based pan and fry the cumin seeds until lightly browned. Add the garlic, ginger and onion and fry until golden brown.

5. Stir in the coriander, garam masala, chilli and green chilli.

6. Turn off the heat, pour the tarka over the cooked dal and serve hot with plain rice, chapati, rayta and stuffed aubergine.

LENTILS, INDIAN CHEESE AND PEAS

Serves 4 - 6

ingredients	Metric	Imperial	American
Moong ki dhuli dal	100 g	4 oz	⅔ cup
Ground turmeric	2.5 ml	½ tsp	½ tsp
Salt to taste			
Water	500 ml	17 fl oz	2¼ cups
TARKA			
Ghee	30 ml	2 tbsp	2 tbsp
Mustard seeds	2.5 ml	½ tsp	½ tsp
Cumin seeds	2.5 ml	½ tsp	½ tsp
Onion seeds	2.5 ml	½ tsp	½ tsp
Garam masala	2.5 ml	½ tsp	½ tsp
PANEER			
Ghee	30 ml	2 tbsp	2 tbsp
Medium onion, finely chopped	1	1	1
Quantity Paneer (see page 94), broken into lumps	1	1	1
Garam masala	2.5 ml	½ tsp	½ tsp
Salt to taste			
PEAS			
Ghee	30 ml	2 tbsp	2 tbsp
Cumin seeds	2.5 ml	½ tsp	½ tsp
Frozen peas, thawed	250 g	9 oz	9 oz
Ground red chilli	2.5 ml	½ tsp	½ tsp
Garam masala	2.5 ml	½ tsp	½ tsp
Salt to taste			
Chopped fresh coriander	30 ml	2 tsp	2 tsp
Lemon juice	15 ml	1 tbsp	1 tbsp

method

1. Place the dal, turmeric, salt and water in a large saucepan and bring to the boil over a medium heat. Skim off any scum, reduce the heat to low, cover and cook for 20 minutes until the dal is tender. Increase the heat and dry off any remaining water.

2. To make the tarka, heat the ghee in a heavy-based pan and fry the mustard, cumin and onion seeds until the mustard seeds start crackling. Stir in the garam masala and add to the cooked dal.

3. To cook the paneer, heat the ghee in a heavy–based pan and fry the onion and paneer over a medium heat until golden brown. Stir in the garam masala and salt and set to one side.

4. To cook the peas, heat the ghee in a heavy-based pan and fry the cumin seeds over a medium heat until browned. Add the peas and spices and cook for 5 minutes or until tender. Stir in the coriander and lemon juice.

5. Reheat the dal, paneer and peas. Place a layer of dal on a serving dish and top with the paneer and the peas. Serve hot with sautéed potatoes, rayta, puri and black eye beans.

GOL GUPPA WITH SAUCE

Makes 24

ingredients

	Metric	Imperial	American
DOUGH			
Brown chapati flour	50 g	2 oz	½ cup
Semolina	25 g	1 oz	3 tbsp
Lemon juice	2.5 ml	½ tsp	½ tsp
Small pinch of salt			
Lukewarm water			
FILLING			
Cooked chick peas (garbanzo beans)	75 g	3 oz	3 oz
Cooked potatoes, peeled and chopped	75 g	3 oz	3 oz
Chopped fresh coriander	15 ml	1 tbsp	1 tbsp
Salt to taste			
Oil for deep-frying			
SAUCE			
Chopped fresh coriander	15 ml	1 tbsp	1 tbsp
Chopped fresh mint	15 ml	1 tbsp	1 tbsp
Water	300 ml	½ pt	1¼ cups
Sugar	10 ml	2 tsp	2 tsp
Garam masala	2.5 ml	½ tsp	½ tsp
Ground red chilli	2.5 ml	½ tsp	½ tsp
Ground roasted cumin	2.5 ml	½ tsp	½ tsp
Tamarind pulp (see page 94)	15 ml	1 tbsp	1 tbsp
Lemon juice	15 ml	1 tbsp	1 tbsp
Salt to taste			

method

1. Mix together all the dough ingredients and knead to a smooth dough. Knead for 3-5 minutes until the dough is springy and satiny. Cover and leave for 30 minutes.

2. Place the filling ingredients in a bowl and mix thoroughly.

3. Roll the dough into a ball with the palm of your hands then flatten it. Place a few drops of oil on the work surface then roll into a thin circle. Cut out several 6 cm/2½ in circles and arrange them on a damp tea towel. Cover with a second damp tea towel and leave to stand for 5 minutes.

4. Heat the oil in a deep frying pan (skillet) over a medium-high heat. Press one circle into the hot oil and as soon as it comes up like a balloon, add another one. Fry 4-5 together until golden brown and crispy, turning frequently. Remove from the heat and leave to cool on a cooling tray.

5. Blend the coriander, mint and 60 ml/4 tbsp of water to a smooth paste in a blender or food processor.

6. Pour the remaining water into a jug and add the remaining sauce ingredients. Mix thoroughly then dilute to taste and chill in the refrigerator for 2-3 hours before using.

7. Make a hole in the centre of each gol guppa and fill it with the filling mixture. Dip it in the sauce and eat it at once so that it is not soggy.

▼

Side Dishes and Snacks

CORN PAKORAS

Makes 12

ingredients

	Metric	Imperial	American
Sweetcorn kernels	150 g	5 oz	5 oz
Water	400 ml	14 fl oz	1⅔ cups
Bread slices	2	2	2
Mashed potatoes	150 g	5 oz	5 oz
Raisins	50 g	2 oz	⅔ cup
Chopped fresh coriander	45 ml	3 tbsp	3 tbsp
Lemon juice	15 ml	1 tbsp	1 tbsp
Garam masala	5 ml	1 tsp	1 tsp
Ground cumin	5 ml	1 tsp	1 tsp
Ground red chilli	5 ml	1 tsp	1 tsp
Small green chilli, chopped	1	1	1
Salt to taste			
Oil for frying			

method

1. Place the corn and water in a pan, bring to the boil and cook for about 3 minutes until tender. Drain well.

2. Dip the bread slices in water for 30 seconds then squeeze out all the water with the palms of your hands. Place the bread in a bowl with the cooked corn and the remaining ingredients. Mix thoroughly then divide into 12 equal portions.

3. Put a few drops of oil on the palm of your hand. Take one portion of the corn mixture and roll it into a smooth round shape. Continue with the remaining pakoras while you heat the oil over a medium heat.

4. Gently slip 6 corn pakoras into the hot oil and fry until golden brown on all sides, turning a few times while cooking.

5. Serve hot with chutney and barfi at tea.

69

SIDE DISHES AND SNACKS

COOKING APPLE BHAJI

Serves 3

ingredients

	Metric	Imperial	American
Oil	45 ml	3 tbsp	3 tbsp
Mustard seeds	5 ml	1 tsp	1 tsp
Ground roasted cumin	5 ml	1 tsp	1 tsp
Garam masala	2.5 ml	½ tsp	½ tsp
Ground turmeric	2.5 ml	½ tsp	½ tsp
Ground red chilli	1.5 ml	¼ tsp	¼ tsp
Ground mace	1.5 ml	¼ tsp	¼ tsp
Ground nutmeg	1.5 ml	¼ tsp	¼ tsp
Salt to taste			
Cooking (tart) apples, peeled, cored and cut into 1 cm/½ in pieces	500 g	18 oz	18 oz
Canned tomatoes	225 g	8 oz	½ lb
Sugar	45 ml	3 tbsp	3 tbsp
Raisins	100 g	4 oz	⅔ cup
GARNISH			
Garam masala	1.5 ml	¼ tsp	¼ tsp
Chopped fresh coriander	15 ml	1 tbsp	1 tbsp
Small green chilli, chopped	1	1	1

method

1. Heat the oil in a heavy-based pan and fry the mustard seeds over a medium heat until they start crackling. Add the cumin, garam masala, turmeric, chilli, mace, nutmeg, salt.

2. Add the apples and tomatoes and fry over a low heat for about 10 minutes until the apples are tender.

3.   Stir in the sugar and raisins, increase the heat and cook until any remaining liquid has evaporated.

4.   Sprinkle over the garnish ingredients and serve hot with puri or paratha, rayta, dal and a kofta dish.

STUFFED CABBAGE LEAVES

(Serves 6)

ingredients

	Metric	Imperial	American
Cabbage leaves	12	12	12
Oil	60 ml	5 tbsp	5 tbsp
Mustard seeds	5 ml	1 tsp	1 tsp
Cumin seeds	5 ml	1 tsp	1 tsp
Potatoes, boiled in their skins then chopped	675 g	1½ lb	1½ lb
Ground coriander	10 ml	2 tsp	2 tsp
Garam masala	5 ml	1 tsp	1 tsp
Ground roasted cumin	5 ml	1 tsp	1 tsp
Ground red chilli	2.5 ml	½ tsp	½ tsp
Ground turmeric	2.5 ml	½ tsp	½ tsp
Ground mace	1.5 ml	¼ tsp	¼ tsp
Ground nutmeg	1.5 ml	¼ tsp	¼ tsp
Salt to taste			
Raisins	100 g	4 oz	⅔ cup
Lemon juice	30 ml	2 tbsp	2 tbsp
Sugar	15 ml	1 tbsp	1 tbsp
Chopped fresh coriander	30 ml	2 tbsp	2 tbsp
Small green chilli, chopped	1	1	1
Oil for frying			

(71)

method

1. Place the cabbage leaves in a pan and just cover with water. Bring to the boil and boil for 2 minutes then drain and leave to dry.

2. Heat the oil and fry the mustard seeds until they start crackling. Add the cumin seeds and fry for a few seconds until lightly browned.

3. Add the potatoes and fry for 10 minutes until lightly browned.

4. Stir in the coriander, garam masala, cumin, chilli, turmeric, mace, nutmeg and salt and cook for 3 minutes over a medium–low heat. Stir in the raisins, lemon juice and sugar and cook for 2 minutes.

5. Turn off the heat and stir in the coriander and chilli.

6. Place spoonfuls of the filling mixture on the centre of the cabbage leaves. Bring in the side edges, roll them into 5 cm/ 2 in parcels and secure with cooks' string.

7. Heat the oil in a deep pan and fry the parcels over a medium heat until light golden brown. Remove with a slotted spoon and drain. Serve hot with chutney at a meal.

CORIANDER POTATOES

Serves 2

ingredients

	Metric	Imperial	American
CHUTNEY			
Bunch of fresh coriander leaves, coarsely chopped	*1*	*1*	*1*
Medium onion, coarsely chopped	*1*	*1*	*1*
Small green chilli	*2*	*1*	*1*
Juice of large lemon	*1*	*1*	*1*
Ground red chilli	*2.5 ml*	*½ tsp*	*½ tsp*
Garam masala	*2.5 ml*	*½ tsp*	*½ tsp*
Salt to taste			
Small new potatoes or potatoes cut into 1 cm/½ in pieces, boiled	*250 g*	*9 oz*	*9 oz*

(73)

method

1. Blend all the chutney ingredients to a fine paste.

2. Mix in the potato pieces and chill for 1-2 hours before serving cold with a meal, or as a snack.

GRATED CAULIFLOWER

Serves 4

ingredients

	Metric	Imperial	American
Oil or ghee	75 ml	5 tbsp	5 tbsp
Mustard seeds	5 ml	1 tsp	1 tsp
Onion seeds	5 ml	1 tsp	1 tsp
Large garlic cloves, crushed	3	3	3
Fresh ginger root, finely chopped	2.5 cm	1 in	1 in
Medium onion, finely chopped	1	1	1
Medium cauliflower, finely grated	1	1	1
Ground coriander	10 ml	2 tsp	2 tsp
Ground roasted cumin	5 ml	1 tsp	1 tsp
Ground red chilli	2.5 ml	½ tsp	½ tsp
Ground turmeric	2.5 ml	½ tsp	½ tsp
Garam masala	2.5 ml	½ tsp	½ tsp
Ground mace	1.5 ml	¼ tsp	¼ tsp
Ground nutmeg	1.5 ml	¼ tsp	¼ tsp
Salt to taste			
GARNISH			
Garam masala	1.5 ml	½ tsp	½ tsp
Chopped fresh coriander	15 ml	1 tbsp	1 tbsp
Small green chilli, chopped	1	1	1

74

method

1. Heat the oil or ghee in a heavy-based pan and fry the mustard seeds until they start crackling. Add the onion seeds and fry for a few seconds until browned.

2. Add the garlic, ginger and onion and fry until lightly browned.

3. Add the cauliflower and cook for 5 minutes.

4. Stir in the cumin, chilli, turmeric, garam masala, mace, nutmeg and salt and mix thoroughly. Reduce the heat to low, cover and cook over a low heat for 20 minutes until tender, stirring occasionally.

5. Sprinkle with the garnish ingredients and serve hot with chapati or puri, rayta and a kofta dish.

ONION AND SPINACH PAKORAS

Serves 4

ingredients

	Metric	Imperial	American
BATTER			
Gram flour, sifted	*250 g*	*9 oz*	*1¼ cups*
Oil	*15 ml*	*1 tbsp*	*1 tbsp*
Chopped fresh coriander	*30 ml*	*2 tbsp*	*2 tbsp*
Dried pomegranate seeds	*15 ml*	*1 tbsp*	*1 tbsp*
Garam masala	*5 ml*	*1 tsp*	*1 tsp*
Ground red chilli	*5 ml*	*1 tsp*	*1 tsp*
Ground roasted cumin	*5 ml*	*1 tsp*	*1 tsp*
Ajowain	*5 ml*	*1 tsp*	*1 tsp*
Small green chilli, chopped	*1*	*1*	*1*
Salt to taste			
Lukewarm water			
VEGETABLES			
Medium onion, thinly sliced	*1*	*1*	*1*
Spinach, chopped	*50 g*	*2 oz*	*2 oz*
Oil for deep-frying			

method

1. Place the flour in a bowl and rub in the oil. Mix in the spices then gradually blend in the water to make a thick batter. Set aside.

2. Stir the onion and spinach into the batter. Heat the oil over a medium heat. Place tablespoonfuls of the mixture into the hot oil, 7 or 8 at a time and fry until golden brown on all sides, pressing and turning them over until cooked.

3. Serve hot at tea with chutney and barfi.

Variations:
Instead of the onions and spinach, use vegetables such as aubergines, carrots, courgette, potato or turnip, thinly sliced or cut into strips. Dip them individually into the batter before frying.

77

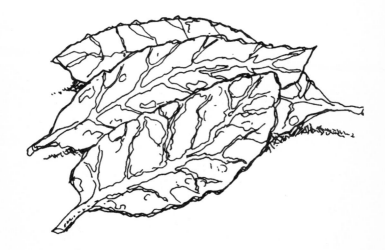

COURGETTE BHAJI

Serves 4

ingredients

	Metric	Imperial	American
Oil or ghee	60 ml	4 tbsp	4 tbsp
Cumin seeds	5 ml	1 tsp	1 tsp
Large garlic cloves, crushed	2	2	2
Fresh ginger root, finely chopped	1 cm	½ in	½ in
Small onion, finely chopped	1 cm	½ in	½ in
Ground coriander	5 ml	1 tsp	1 tsp
Garam masala	2.5 ml	½ tsp	½ tsp
Ground turmeric	2.5 ml	½ tsp	½ tsp
Ground red chilli	1.5 ml	¼ tsp	¼ tsp
Salt to taste			
Courgettes (zucchini), cut into 1 cm/½ in pieces	500 g	18 oz	18 oz
Canned tomatoes	225 g	8 oz	½ lb
GARNISH			
Garam masala	1.5 ml	¼ tsp	¼ tsp
Chopped fresh coriander	15 ml	1 tbsp	1 tbsp
Small green chilli, chopped	1	1	1

method

1. Heat the oil or ghee in a heavy-based pan and fry the cumin seeds until lightly browned.

2. Add the garlic, ginger and onion and fry until lightly browned.

3. Add the coriander, garam masala, turmeric, chilli, salt, courgettes and tomatoes, bring to the boil, cover and cook over a low heat for about 20 minutes until tender, stirring occasionally.

4. Increase the heat and dry off any remaining liquid.

5. Sprinkle with the garnish ingredients and serve hot with lentil, chapati and rayta.

MARROW BHAJI

Serves 4

ingredients

	Metric	Imperial	American
Oil or ghee	75 ml	5 tbsp	5 tbsp
Mustard seeds	5 ml	1 tsp	1 tsp
Onion seeds	5 ml	1 tsp	1 tsp
Small onion, finely chopped	1	1	1
Fresh ginger root	1 cm	½ in	½ in
Ground coriander	5 ml	1 tsp	1 tsp
Ground roasted cumin	5 ml	1 tsp	1 tsp
Ground red chilli	2.5 ml	½ tsp	½ tsp
Ground turmeric	2.5 ml	½ tsp	½ tsp
Garam masala	2.5 ml	½ tsp	½ tsp
Salt to taste			
Marrow (squash), peeled and cut into 1 cm/½ in cubes	900 g	2 lb	2 lb
Water	100 ml	3½ fl oz	6½ tbsp
GARNISH			
Garam masala	2.5 ml	½ tsp	½ tsp
Chopped fresh coriander	15 ml	1 tbsp	1 tbsp
Small green chilli, chopped	1	1	1

1. Heat the oil or ghee in a heavy–based pan and fry the mustard seeds over a medium heat until they start crackling. Stir in the onion seeds and fry for a few seconds until lightly browned.

2. Stir in the onion and ginger and fry until lightly browned.

3. Add the coriander, cumin, chilli, turmeric, garam masala and salt. Stir in the marrow and water and bring to the boil. Reduce the heat, cover and cook for 30 minutes until the marrow is tender, stirring occasionally.

4. Increase the heat and dry off any remaining water.

5. Sprinkle with the garnish ingredients and serve hot with dal and rice.

MARROW KEBAB

ingredients

Makes 14

	Metric	Imperial	American
Marrow (squash), peeled and grated	900 g	2 lb	2 lb
Water	100 ml	3½ fl oz	6½ tbsp
Gram flour	50 g	2 oz	½ cup
Chopped fresh coriander	45 ml	3 tbsp	3 tbsp
Small green chilli, chopped	1	1	1
Garam masala	5 ml	1 tsp	1 tsp
Ground roasted cumin	5 ml	1 tsp	1 tsp
Ground red chilli	1.5 ml	¼ tsp	¼ tsp
Ground mace	1.5 ml	¼ tsp	¼ tsp
Ground nutmeg	1.5 ml	¼ tsp	¼ tsp
Salt to taste			
Almonds, blanched	14	14	14
Cashew nuts	14	14	14
Raisins	50 g	2 oz	⅔ cup
Oil for frying			

method

1. Cook the marrow and water for 15 minutes until tender then drain well. Place in a strainer and squeeze out all the water.

2. Lightly sift the gram flour and brown it in a dry frying pan (skillet) on a low heat.

3. Place the marrow in a bowl and stir in the gram flour, coriander, chilli, garam masala, cumin, chilli, mace, nutmeg and salt. Mix thoroughly and divide into 14 equal portions.

4. Put an almond, a cashew nut and a few raisins in the centre of each portion, bring the edges over the cover and make it into a round shape. Repeat until you have made all the kebabs.

5. Meanwhile, heat the oil in a heavy-based pan, then gently slip the kebabs into the pan and fry until golden brown.

6. Serve hot with chutney for tea, or with pulao at a meal.

81

POTATO PATTIES

Makes 12

	ingredients		
	Metric	Imperial	American
POTATO MIXTURE			
Mashed potatoes	*450 g*	*1 lb*	*1 lb*
Chopped fresh coriander	*15 ml*	*1 tbsp*	*1 tbsp*
Pomegranate seeds	*5 ml*	*1 tsp*	*1 tsp*
Garam masala	*2.5 ml*	*½ tsp*	*½ tsp*
Ground red chilli	*2.5 ml*	*½ tsp*	*½ tsp*
Ground roasted cumin	*2.5 ml*	*½ tsp*	*½ tsp*
Small green chilli, chopped (optional)	*1*	*1*	*1*
Salt to taste			
PEA FILLING			
Oil	*30 ml*	*2 tbsp*	*2 tbsp*
Mustard seeds	*2.5 ml*	*½ tsp*	*½ tsp*
Cumin seeds	*2.5 ml*	*½ tsp*	*½ tsp*
Ground roasted cumin	*5 ml*	*1 tsp*	*1 tsp*
Ground red chilli	*1.5 ml*	*¼ tsp*	*¼ tsp*
Ground turmeric	*1.5 ml*	*¼ tsp*	*¼ tsp*
Salt to taste			
Frozen peas, thawed	*250 g*	*9 oz*	*9 oz*
Lemon juice	*30 ml*	*2 tbsp*	*2 tbsp*
Chopped fresh coriander	*15 ml*	*1 tbsp*	*1 tbsp*
Garam masala	*5 ml*	*1 tsp*	*1 tsp*
Oil for frying			

method

1. Place the potato mixture ingredients in a bowl and blend thoroughly. Divide into 12 equal portions.

2. To make the filling, heat the oil in a heavy-based pan and fry the mustard seeds until they start crackling. Add the cumin seeds and fry for a few seconds until lightly browned. Stir in the cumin, chilli, turmeric and salt. Stir in the peas and cook for about 5 minutes until the peas are cooked.

3. Add the lemon juice coriander and garam masala, remove from the heat and divide the mixture into 12 equal portions.

4. Take one portion of potato and roll it into a ball. Flatten the ball and place a portion of the pea mixture in the centre. Bring the edges over and smoothly cover the filling. Roll into a ball again and flatten until it is a 1 cm/½ in thick circle. Repeat with the remaining mixture.

5. Heat a flat frying pan (skillet) over a medium heat and smear with 30 ml/2 tbsp of oil. Place 5-6 patties on it and fry until golden brown. Turn them over carefully, pour 30 ml/2 tbsp of oil around the patties and fry the other side until golden brown.

6. Serve hot with chutney for tea.

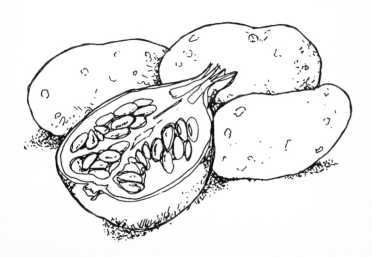

FRIED POTATOES IN SPICY SAUCE

ingredients

Serves 4

	Metric	Imperial	American
Small potatoes	500 g	18 oz	18 oz
Ghee or oil	120 ml	4 fl oz	½ cup
Small onion, finely chopped	1	1	1
Cloves	4	4	4
Peppercorns	4	4	4
Bay leaves	2	2	2
Cardamom pod	1	1	1
Cinnamon stick	1 cm	½ in	½ in
Large onion, cut into chunks	1	1	1
Large garlic cloves	3	3	3
Fresh ginger root	1 cm	½ in	½ in
Ground coriander	10 ml	2 tsp	2 tsp
Ground roasted cumin	2.5 ml	½ tsp	½ tsp
Ground red chilli	2.5 ml	½ tsp	½ tsp
Ground turmeric	2.5 ml	½ tsp	½ tsp
Salt to taste			
Canned tomatoes	400 g	14 oz	14 oz
Natural yoghurt	150 ml	¼ pt	⅔ cup
Water	375 ml	13 fl oz	1½ cups
GARNISH			
Garam masala	2.5 ml	½ tsp	½ tsp
Chopped fresh coriander	15 ml	1 tbsp	1 tbsp
Small green chilli, chopped	1	1	1

method

1. Prick the potatoes all over with a fork. Heat half the ghee or oil and fry the potatoes until golden brown on all sides. Drain and set aside.

2. Heat the remaining ghee or oil in a heavy-based pan and fry the chopped onion, cloves, peppercorns, bay leaves, cardamom and cinnamon over a medium heat until golden brown.

3. Blend the onion, garlic and ginger to a smooth paste. Stir into the pan and fry until golden brown.

4. Stir in the coriander, cumin, chilli, turmeric and salt. Stir in the tomatoes and cook until the ghee appears on top of the mixture.

5. Stir in the yoghurt and cook until all the liquid has been absorbed.

6. Add the water and fried potatoes, bring to the boil then cover and cook gently for about 20 minutes until tender. (If you are not serving the dish with rice, reduce the quantity of water to 200 ml/7 fl oz/scant 1 cup.)

7. Sprinkle over the garnish ingredients and serve hot.

STUFFED POTATOES

Serves 4 - 6

ingredients

	Metric	Imperial	American
Medium potatoes	1 kg	2 lb	2 lb
Oil	75 ml	5 tbsp	5 tbsp
Mustard seeds	5 ml	1 tsp	1 tsp
Garam masala	5 ml	1 tsp	1 tsp
Ground coriander	5 ml	1 tsp	1 tsp
Ground roasted cumin	5 ml	1 tsp	1 tsp
Ground red chilli	2.5 ml	½ tsp	½ tsp
Ground turmeric	2.5 ml	½ tsp	½ tsp
Salt to taste			
Mixed vegetables, frozen or boiled	250 g	9 oz	9 oz
Raisins	100 g	4 oz	⅔ cup
Chopped fresh coriander	30 ml	2 tbsp	2 tbsp
Small green chilli, chopped	1	1	1
Oil for frying	75 ml	5 tbsp	5 tbsp

method

1. Boil the potatoes in their skins, peel them and divide them in half. Chop half. Slice 3 mm/⅛ in off the top of the other half and scoop out as much as possible from the potatoes.

2. Heat the oil in a heavy-based pan and fry the mustard seeds until they start crackling. Add the chopped potatoes and fry over a medium-low heat for about 10 minutes until light golden brown.

3. Stir in the garam masala, coriander, cumin, chilli, turmeric and salt. Stir in the vegetables and cook for 7 minutes.

4. Stir in the raisins, coriander and chilli. Remove from the heat.

5. Stuff the whole potatoes with the mixture and replace the tops.

6. Heat the oil and fry the stuffed potatoes over a medium heat for about 10 minutes until crispy golden brown on all sides.

7. Serve hot with chutney, puri, dal, yoghurt and a kofta dish.

ONION PARATHA

Makes 12

ingredients

	Metric	Imperial	American
Chapati flour	*550 g*	*1¼ lb*	*5 cups*
Medium onion, finely chopped	*1*	*1*	*1*
Small green chilli, finely chopped	*1*	*1*	*1*
Chopped fresh coriander	*30 ml*	*2 tbsp*	*2 tbsp*
Oil	*15 ml*	*1 tbsp*	*1 tbsp*
Garam masala	*5 ml*	*1 tsp*	*1 tsp*
Ajowain	*5 ml*	*1 tsp*	*1 tsp*
Ground red chilli	*2.5 ml*	*½ tsp*	*½ tsp*
Salt to taste			
Lukewarm water	*250 ml*	*8 fl oz*	*1 cup*
Oil for frying			
Butter or ghee			

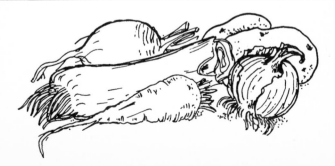

method

1. Place 500 g/18 oz/4½ cups of flour in a large bowl and add the onion, chilli, coriander, oil, and spices. Gradually blend in the water to make a soft dough. Knead for 5 minutes until the dough is springy and satiny. Cover and leave for 30 minutes.

2. While the frying pan (skillet) is heating, divide the dough into 12 equal portions and roll them into balls, dust with flour and flatten into circles.

3. Smear half of the circles with butter or ghee and fold in half. Smear the half again and fold again into a triangle. Sprinkle with flour and roll out to 2.5 mm/⅛ in thick, keeping the triangular shape.

4. Place the paratha on the hot frying pan (skillet) and cook both sides dry like a chapati. Then pour 10 ml/2 tsp of oil over it and fry the first side until lightly browned. Make 6 or 7 slits on the paratha and pour on some more oil. Fry the other side until light golden.

5. Serve hot with pickle, butter and natural yoghurt.

COLOURED RICE

Serves 4

ingredients

	Metric	Imperial	American
Ghee	90 ml	6 tbsp	6 tbsp
Cumin seeds	5 ml	1 tsp	1 tsp
Cloves	5	5	5
Peppercorns	5	5	5
Bay leaves	2	2	2
Cinnamon stick	2.5 cm	1 in	1 in
Black cardamom pod	1	1	1
Medium onion, thinly sliced	1	1	1
Patna or basmati rice, washed and drained	225 g	8 oz	1 cup
Large garlic cloves, crushed	2	2	2
Garam masala	5 ml	1 tsp	1 tsp
Salt to taste			
Frozen peas, thawed	225 g	8 oz	½ lb
Water	500 ml	17 fl oz	2¼ cups
Red food colour	1.5 ml	¼ tsp	¼ tsp
Yellow food colour	5 ml	1 tsp	1 tsp

89

method

1. Heat the ghee in a heavy-based pan and fry the cumin seeds until lightly browned. Add the cloves, peppercorns, bay leaves, cinnamon, cardamom, onion and garlic and fry until golden brown.

2. Mix in the drained rice and fry for 2 minutes.

3. Stir in the garam masala, salt, peas and water. Bring to the boil, reduce the heat to low, cover and cook for 15 minutes. If any water is left, dry off on a high heat but don't stir; tip the pan to check the water.

4. Turn off the heat. Mix the red colour into one side of the rice with a fork and the yellow colour into the other side. Cover and leave for 5 minutes for serving hot with rayta and cauliflower.

PLAIN RICE

ingredients

Serves 4 - 6

	Metric	Imperial	American
Patna or basmati rice, washed and drained	250 g	9 oz	1 cup
Water	750 ml	1¼ pts	3 cups
Ghee	15 ml	1 tbsp	1 tbsp

method

1. Place the rice, water and ghee in a pan and bring to the boil over a medium heat.

2. Reduce the heat to low, cover the pan and cook for 15 minutes. If any water is left, dry it off on a high heat but don't stir.

3. Turn off the heat and leave for at least 5 minutes before serving. Separate the grains with a fork and serve hot with dal, curries, yoghurt and pickle.

TOMATO, CUCUMBER AND ONION RAYTA

Serves 4

ingredients

	Metric	Imperial	American
Natural yoghurt	500 g	17 fl oz	2¼ cups
Tomatoes, cut into 1 cm/½ in pieces	150 g	5 oz	5 oz
Small onion, finely chopped	1	1	1
Cucumber, cut into 1 cm/½ in pieces	½	½	½
Salt to taste			
Ground roasted cumin			
GARNISH			
Ground roasted cumin	2.5 ml	½ tsp	½ tsp
Chopped fresh coriander	15 ml	1 tbsp	1 tsp
Small green chilli, chopped	1	1	1

91

method

1. Whisk the yoghurt until smooth. Stir in the tomatoes, onion, cucumber, salt and cumin. Chill in the refrigerator.

2. Sprinkle with the garnish ingredients before serving.

MARROW RAYTA

Serves 4

ingredients

	Metric	Imperial	American
Marrow (squash), peeled and grated	250 g	9 oz	9 oz
Water	300 ml	½ pt	1¼ cups
Natural yoghurt	450 ml	⅔ pt	2 cups
Salt to taste			
GARNISH			
Ground roasted cumin	5 ml	1 tsp	1 tsp
Chopped fresh coriander	30 ml	2 tbsp	2 tbsp
Small green chilli, chopped	1	1	1

92

method

1. Place the marrow and water in a pan over a medium heat and cook for 10 minutes until tender. Strain through a colander, squeezing out excess water with your hands.

2. Place the yoghurt in a bowl and whisk with a fork until smooth. Add the marrow, salt and half the garnish ingredients.

3. Chill in the refrigerator for 2-3 hours before serving sprinkled with the remaining garnish.

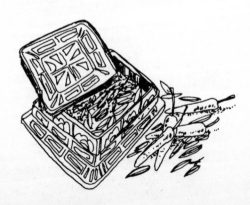

▼
Miscellaneous

GARAM MASALA

Makes 100 g/4 oz

ingredients

	Metric	Imperial	American
Black cardamom seeds	25 g	1 oz	1 oz
Cloves	25 g	1 oz	1 oz
Cinnamon stick, crushed	25 g	1 oz	1 oz
Peppercorns	25 g	1 oz	1 oz

method

1. Grind all the ingredients together in a coffee grinder until they form a fine powder.
2. Store in an airtight container.

TAMARIND PULP

Makes about 75 g/3 oz

ingredients

	Metric	Imperial	American
Dry tamarind	100 g	4 oz	¼ lb
Water	300 ml	½ pt	1¼ cups

method

1. Place the tamarind and water in a pan and bring to the boil. Boil for 15 minutes over a medium-low heat until soft.

2. Sieve the pulp from the tamarind and discard the seeds and sticks; this should not exceed 15 ml/1 tbsp.

QUICK KHOYA

Makes about 75 g/3 oz

ingredients

	Metric	Imperial	American
Full cream milk powder	50 g	2 oz	½ cup
Ghee, melted	10 ml	2 tsp	2 tsp
Lukewarm milk	30 ml	2 tbsp	2 tbsp

method

1. Combine all the ingredients in a bowl until a soft dough forms.

PANEER – INDIAN CHEESE

Makes about 225 g/8 oz

ingredients

	Metric	Imperial	American
Gold top milk	*1.2 l*	*2 pts*	*5 cups*
Lemon juice	*30 ml*	*2 tbsp*	*2 tbsp*

method

1. Bring the milk to the boil. Add the lemon juice so that the milk separates into curds and whey. Add a little more if necessary to achieve this. Leave to set for 5 minutes.

2. Line a strainer with a muslin (cheesecloth) cloth and strain the milk. Reserve the whey to use in curries instead of water to add extra flavour and minerals.

3. Squeeze the excess whey out of the curd and fold the cloth around the paneer to form a square about 10 cm/4 in.

4. Place the paneer on an upturned plate and place a heavy weight on top to squeeze out excess whey. Leave for about 4 hours to set.

Index